MOVING FORWARD

To my editor, Jessica Pearse. This book would be nothing without you.

To my family, my friends, and my acquaintances who continue to be there for me, no matter what. This one's for all of you.

To my cats, Sid and Nancy, my two favorite snuggle bugs.

(Unfortunately, they're illiterate, so they'll never know this acknowledgment exists. But it's the thought that counts, right?)

Disclaimer, revised

I'm going to fill this disclaimer out a bit more than with my first book. As before, this book is not intended to be a guide. As I stated before, this book also is not intended to be an answer to all of your problems. That is still something you have to figure out on your own. I stand by this, because I am only speaking from my own unique human experience, and for what has worked for me. This shouldn't be scary— this should be empowering. You are in control of your own world, and you have the power to make it as great as you want it to be. I still hope you are able to get something from what I've learned, and what I'm still working through.

I also want to mention that, as with any book, this is how I'm feeling now. It's very possible I will look at this book in 10 years and argue with myself. Already, reading through my first book, there are things that I don't agree with (and I'm the author). I'm okay with this.

My goal with this book is to capture where I am at in my own mental journey, right now, in 2018. I hope that this resonates with you, and I hope you are able to gain something from what I've learned in the past year.

FOREWORD

Well, here I am. Again.

As I'm writing this on November 4, 2018, I've just gotten back to Milwaukee—from visiting New Orleans to speak with their National Alliance on Mental Illness (NAMI) chapter and do a few signings there. The month before, I was in New York City to speak with their NAMI chapter, and I did a signing there as well. So far, so good.

For my first book's tour, I've decided to return to the 10 cities I mentioned in the book, and give back to their local NAMI chapters. It's not the most lucrative tour for me, by any means, but it feels right, and I'm lucky I still have my remote job so I can support myself on the road. It's not easy—but I'm learning how to sustainably balance the two as I continue to travel.

I'm traveling toward *where* I want to go, following a journey of personal growth rather than retreating further into my past memories. Part of this means taking time in each city I visit, and part means traveling with intent and purpose. This is a daily struggle, still, but I can feel myself growing stronger with each city and with each experience. I feel myself growing more stable, more secure, more focused on where I'd like to be—an unencumbered future.

This personal progression was my goal at the end of my first book, so I'm proud of this. I don't mean to get too sappy, but I've never felt more motivated or driven in my life, which to me, is much better than being simply "happy," as was my goal before. I not only feel better, but I see a world beyond my hardships, and I'm growing my world further than I ever could have imagined. I truly believe this is because I learned to share my story, to open up to others, and to truly listen to others' stories—to gain perspective with each person I met, and to ultimately transcend those dark times in my past.

I did see All Them Witches and Handsome Jack while I was in New Orleans, and I did still give one ticket away. That's more because, well, they both just released great albums this year (2018), and I've decided that this ticket thing is a really fun thing to do. It's something I'd like to continue doing when I have the money for it. I like to give someone else that experience, and I like knowing that the person has no idea where the ticket came from. I love this—a faceless good deed that I hope the person will perpetuate past the show. I'm a sucker for it.

While I did have a beer while I was there, I drank water outside of that, which (as you may know from the first book) would have been incredibly difficult for me to do a year ago. Moderation was not my forte, to say the least, but I'm getting better at this. I think this might be because my pain is no longer a cinder block lodged in the center of my mind. Because I'm calmer mentally, I'm less focused on flushing this block from my thoughts—now, they flow in sync with my actions, at least mostly. At least much better than before.

While these might not seem like massive steps, for me, I'm proud of where I am now. And while there is still room for growth (as I believe there always is, no matter where you are in life), where I am is sustainable. And I'm grateful for that. I'm grateful I could move on from where I was in even the final pages of my first book, and I'm grateful that now I'm heading in a much more positive direction.

If I'm doing so much better, then why am I doing this? Well, after re-reading my first book (call me narcissistic; I'll take it), I realized I've traveled so much further in my mental health journey, far past the final pages of my first book. I've decided to continue past the physical journey, to shed light upon the mental journey I went on after my physical one was complete.

As I mentioned in my first book—the body can heal itself, but the mind cannot, not unless you actively focus on positive improvement. While for me, I currently do not need therapy or medication, I have not put it off the table completely. If you are in a similar situation, I want you to understand that I'm not against those things at all, and I acknowledge that if I do need them in the future, they'll be welcomed with open arms (and hopefully my insurance will welcome it, too. If not, I'm glad to know that NAMI provides so many great, free group sessions in the meantime). Mental health is more important than any sort of rules I've constructed in my head, and that's at the top of my list of takeaways from last year. I've learned that this journey is fluid, is constant, is without expiration—and I've grown to accept that.

I've come to realize that this journey is dynamic. I still have flashbacks, I still have bad days, and I still have regressions. But for now, I'm able to move past them and lead a relatively normal and fulfilling life. It's still not perfect, but I'm grateful for where I am now.

In this book, I hope to welcome you into the world of my greater mental journey, beyond my physical "manic quest for reason," as I like to call it. I'll share with you what I've done to keep myself on track, what I still struggle with, and where I hope to be in years to come. I've also included some other essays that have been important to my own personal growth—past the struggles I mentioned in my first book.

This book can either be read from front to back, or you can skip to certain sections, as they are stand-alone essays. You can also read from back to front, or only odd pages, or only read pages with your favorite words on them (but I wouldn't recommend it). Above all, however you choose to read this, I hope you are able to take something from this, and I hope reading this helps you as much as writing it helped me.

Cheers,

Becky

Our better natures seek elevation
A refuge for the coming night
No one gets to their heaven without a fight
-Rush, "Armor and Sword"

Chapter One
(Sustainably) Moving Forward

In my first book, I wouldn't exactly call myself a shining beacon of optimism. While re-reading even two months after *This Road Must Go Somewhere* was published, there were often times where I cringed to myself, either internally saying *wow, that's rough* or *wow, way to be a bitch, Becky*. (I admit this is a bit harsh, but we are all our own toughest critics.) As I'm slowly getting back to optimism, I look back on these times, squinting to make out what I was thinking while walking through these shadows. It's difficult to re-read through these times in my past and confidently say I'd react the same way as the person I've grown into now. I'm grateful for that.

Though often agonizing to read, I stand by those times and what I wrote, even if it was sometimes painfully raw and visceral. It's honest and real to what I was feeling at that time.

It still surprises me what I went through—it still seems surreal to me, even now. It would be disconcerting if I bounced back gracefully. I think I would be more worried if I hadn't stumbled, if I hadn't challenged these thoughts in my head, if I hadn't spent time clawing at the walls from the bottom of a well before I finally asked for a ladder. And if I hadn't fallen off that ladder a few times, refused it again, told whoever threw it down to fuck off, then spent more time clawing the walls before sheepishly asking someone to throw down a ladder? I don't know where I'd be.

But was I preemptive in saying *this is the end of my journey*? Absolutely. At the end of my first book, it was only the beginning of my sustainable mental journey toward recovery. Even as I start this book, I know I still have a long way to go. This isn't a typical story where the protagonist encounters a problem, goes through a novel's worth of hardship, then defeats the problem at the end. As I learned in 2017, there is no magical ending. It continues to be a lot of hard, behind-the-scenes work to get to where I am today, and I'm grateful that I had the endurance to do it all and continue pushing forward and climbing upward, with the help of those around me.

I acknowledge that this will be something that I carry with me for the rest of my life. As I learned in my first book, however, this does not have to be an overwhelmingly heavy weight. That it is not a burden to carry on my own. Sure, the stoic mask looks cool, in theory, almost James Bond–esque, but the real, visceral, vulnerable face behind that mask is still there. This mask is so much more transparent than I originally thought, especially after talking with those I care about most, those who saw me endure these times and are still there for me. Like trying to cover up zits with a lightweight, eco-friendly, mineral-based foundation I recently purchased, you can still see the blemishes underneath.

As you may have gathered from my first book, I left off realizing that to build any sort of recovery, I would have to rebuild my base again—meaning I would have to learn how to reenter society, learn how to rebuild relationships, and learn how to sustainably keep on keepin' on. At the end of my first book, the foundation I stood upon was shaky. I was actively trying to move forward, but with every step I took, the ground was crumbling beneath my feet, and I would fall back to the starting line. And with every trip I took, I learned something, yes, but it was almost like I was in *Groundhog Day*, the 1990s Bill Murray movie where every day was the same but also different in that there was frustration—that nothing was changing, and with every day came a different reaction. All Them Witches concerts became my Punxsutawney, Pennsylvania. With each concert (while I adore them as people as well as for their music), I became more and more frustrated that nothing was changing, that I wasn't moving forward, no matter how hard I actively tried.

To be clear, this was my fault, not theirs. They're lovely.

While it was a constant, it wasn't a stable base because it wasn't sustainable. There was no maintainable way that I could go to an All Them Witches concert whenever I was feeling down. If anything, I hope they're not touring that much, because that sounds exhausting and I want them to be well. But also for me, I needed to stop running, and I needed to learn how to reenter the world as a productive human being. I think this goes with anything—had I not chosen All Them Witches concerts, I could have simply chosen to drink alone in my apartment. I was definitely on the path to do so, and I easily could have fallen in that direction. This could have equally been my *Groundhog Day.* It could have been waking up and pouring a liberal shot of whiskey in my coffee, with my temples throbbing from the night before (or even worse, still dulled by alcohol).

This *sustainability* is where true recovery comes in. I could not continually attend All Them Witches concerts, just as I could not continually destroy my liver. While I felt better at the time, and while I would still argue that overall All Them Witches music has positively impacted my life, and that alcohol in moderation can be okay, it was my *expectations* for these things. I expected them to heal me, but only I could heal myself.

Past my own recovery, I needed to be a productive member of society again—for myself and for others. I couldn't wait for this to happen, because only I could make this a reality.

At first, I was productive for others. I acknowledged that they were worried about me, and I wanted to be sure they didn't have to anymore. But as I learned how to interact with society again, this shifted and leveled to a balanced "for them, and for me."

This was difficult.

For me, I've always struggled with giving too much to others while sacrificing my own well-being. I needed to relearn how to interact with people, how to rebuild relationships with those who I would encounter every day. I needed to learn how to own where I was, to trust others enough around me to open up to them, and to learn how to take advice again. I needed to be at a point where I would be able to give them advice, too, which meant clearing my head and processing the thoughts that had festered in my mind for far too long.

This give and take, for me, is how sustainability is built again. That's how I build trust—through this honest, maskless exchange of stories and hardships. Often times, I am able to learn more about myself when I give my honest advice to others, and I hope those around me experience the same when they give me advice. But this equal balance— of caring for myself while also caring for others—is important.

And do I have trust issues now? You betcha. But with each person I learn to trust, those issues are slowly dissipating. I first was concerned that those who loved me would judge me, or treat me differently, but I learned most of those I truly trust and cherish still accepted me for who I was, even then—and for who I am now. I learned that it felt so much better to be honest and open about how I felt.

Of course, they still give me shit for how I reacted after it all happened, but I'd expect nothing less. If they pretended like it was completely normal and didn't check me for the absolutely ridiculous things I did, I'm not sure I would trust their judgment.

There is a stark difference between those who judge silently and those who joke openly—the jokers openly want me to do better, and the judgers are not in it for my best interests. That's okay—I've learned that I am in control, for the most part, of those who I choose to allow in my social circle. This isn't selfish because I'm building my tribe, and I'm grateful for the badass one I've been able to gather. I'm grateful that they've accepted me, too, rather than questioning whether they'll end up leaving me high and dry—or even worse, before I'd run away without giving them a chance to prove me wrong.

Those who care about me most and those who are *sustainably* there for me will appreciate if I am open and honest versus pretending behind the stoic mask I puppeted before—they are helping me build that base. With those who judged me or treated me differently, often times, these relationships weren't ever sustainable, so I learned to politely weed those out. And as I learned in the first book, while I can't make everyone happy without losing myself completely—there's also no reason to be a jerk to anyone.

As someone who has been individualistic to a fault, this was an especially difficult lesson to learn, one I continue to learn as I grow as an adult. It seems strange to say, "To be an individual, you have to learn how to trust people." Again, think of it as your base. Even the most unique houses need some sort of foundation—your social circle is just that. It is not weak to rely on them as long as you continue to take care of yourself. This equilibrium between sharing and giving is where that foundation turns from plywood to concrete. I'm grateful I learned this now, and I'm grateful for the people who have taught me that this is okay. If you're constantly tearing yourself down, there is no way you can sustainably build anything. You can only start to build if you accept the tools you're given—you cannot rebuild on your own. These external philosophies, meshed with your own internal philosophies, build a sustainable base where you can actually continue to grow. I still have a long way to go, as I mentioned before. However, through this exchange of philosophies—be it from great friends, my family, or great books—I feel myself growing stronger and steadier. My platform is stable, and it is fertile.

Chapter Two
"Hi, I'm Becky, and I Almost Became an Alcoholic"

One of the biggest reviews of my first book was, "Wow, you sure drank a lot." I think that came as a surprise to those who knew me best, as under normal circumstances, I was usually able to control it.

Alcohol was always something I've used as a placeholder drug. Whenever I was uncomfortable, I'd have a beer to ease my nerves. If I wasn't feeling sociable, I'd have a beer to loosen up. When my thoughts and my depression got to be too much, *drink*, I thought, just like playing a warped drinking game.

Every time you feel sad or bad, drink.

It wasn't the physical substance I was addicted to at that point—it was how it made me feel, and it blocked out those demons. But physical addiction could have easily been my next step—I was inches away. I knew I needed to stop before the physical grip became real, before my hands would shake uncontrollably if I couldn't have a whiskey-ginger or gin and tonic. This could have been anything—I could have latched onto another drug or simply another unhealthy habit to mask my already unhealthy mental state. I chose alcohol because, simply put, it's one of the most socially acceptable drugs to abuse, and it's easily accessible.

Reviewing my journals now, I can tell I recognized the problem, even subconsciously, because as best I could, I covered it up. It's difficult to retroactively analyze myself, but I think this is why I kept most of my drinking to my own home, and cities where I didn't know anyone, or designated "celebration" times. Though I didn't fully realize it at the time, I was not being easy on my body. I was taking the easy way out, the weak way out—and ultimately, I felt physically and emotionally exhausted from hiding from my feelings. I was ashamed.

Again, I was weak then. Because I had grown accustomed to this weakness, I grew used to being weak instead of challenging and trying to solve my problems. This became homeostasis and routine, which makes it much more difficult to see a problem. This was probably due to being in a perpetual state of hung-over-ness and being caught in the moment—the alcohol freed my mind enough to open my thoughts, but because my thoughts weren't clear, I couldn't work through them. I was simply reliving the moments in my head as they had been, without the ability to think of solutions. I recognized it was a problem, but because I didn't take the time to fix it, this problem became my homeostasis. My unstable vice invaded my mental home, and it trashed it.

I'm not sure I would have recognized just how bad I was until I took the time to study it, to analyze it, to summarize it after living it. I didn't give myself time to process because I was eroding my brain into submission. I beat up my brain and dragged it with me wherever I went—half-functional, half-awake.

I often say the best therapy I could have done was to write my last book, which included diving deep into the volumes of diary entries I wrote during that year—much like looking at old pictures, realizing that the punk phase you went through in high school really was as embarrassing and awkward as your mother said it was. You can't truly see the full reality of these flaws until you examine them later, until you review the highlights instead of getting caught in the minutiae. While I was in it, I didn't realize how bad it was until I mapped it out on paper and summarized it.

After family members read my first book, I learned that alcoholism is something that runs strong in my family. I'm not about to outline who in my family suffered and still does suffer, but it's telling that I had no idea they were suffering until they told me, or until I had been told by other family members. Especially in Milwaukee, where beer is not only a pastime but also so heavily tied to our culture, it easily becomes a routine to those who live here. Everything *but* the bars shut down around 9:00 pm in Milwaukee, meaning that if you want to have a social life after work, the alcohol scene is difficult to avoid. The rhetoric in this city is that if you want to unwind, you have a beer. If you have a problem, you have a beer. I had to rewrite this rhetoric in my head—I had to learn to kill this *alcohol as medicine* mentality from its root. It is not as cool as Dean Martin made it look—in reality, it's a crutch that, the more you lean on it, will only make you weaker.

Once I learned to combat the problems I was covering with alcohol, my attitude toward alcohol shifted too, and again, this is another thing that worked for me but may not work for you. For me, because I caught it early enough, I was able to cut it out completely for a month. This actually came from a brief conversation I had with Robby, the drummer from All Them Witches, where he told me in passing that he cut out alcohol for a month. I thought, "Well, if he can do that on the road, I can do that in my own life, too."

At first, it was isolating. I feared people would judge me if I was at a bar without a beer in hand. I feared that I wouldn't be accepted by those who I had gone out with before. I feared I would be labeled as boring—the proverbial *wet blanket*. I avoided the bars, thinking they were simply a place I didn't belong anymore.

But again, as I mentioned before, there is literally no other place open past 9:00 pm, and I work from home; eventually, I had to combat this fear head on if I wanted to maintain a social life. A month seems short on paper, but in practice, it can seem like an eternity—especially when you don't get out much to begin with.

What I learned? Usually, nobody cared if I drank or not. And if someone did say something judgmental? It's incredibly easy to dismiss this unnecessary judgment. Also, water is great, and waking up hydrated is *way* better than waking up hungover. If I wake up after a traumatic dream, it's easier to move forward healthfully if my temples aren't throbbing from the night before (also, strangely, my traumatic dreams happen less often, but maybe that's because I'm actually working through my problems).

Once the month was done, I'm fortunate that I was able to casually drink once a week, in moderation, and only in social settings where I knew those around me. Now, I actually appreciate what I'm drinking, instead of downing the cheapest gin and tonics whatever bar has to offer.

Now, sometimes I even get a seltzer and lime, which is something I never in a million years saw myself doing. Once alcohol was no longer my necessary crutch, my attitude toward it shifted. Now, I'm fine with one beer, if any, and I'm sure my liver and my bank account are forever grateful. Once I learned how to walk without this crutch—once I learned how to combat these thoughts in my head—I was able to return to appreciating in moderation.

Past the social aspect, I also had to learn how to address alone times without a full glass of my precious boxed wine. I used to call it "my muse, on tap." Even after I stopped relying on alcohol socially, it had become an integral part of my writing process over the years. It helped me loosen the ideas from my head, and it gave me confidence to put them on the page. But now? I'm proud to say that I wrote this book 100% sober, which unfortunately, was not the case with my first book.

It's difficult to write sober, at least for me, because I had always followed the Hemingway trope to "write drunk, edit sober." As a writer, drinking is so heavily intertwined with the writing process, even if it's just following the patterns of other writers. I really did not choose the right creative path to cut back drinking with, but now that I've mostly cut it out while writing, I feel it's much easier to write without it—I feel like my thoughts flow much more smoothly and words come out easier. This is probably from three things: (1) learning how to address my thoughts, (2) learning how to open up with others without alcohol, and (3) knowing that my brain works much better when I'm not dulling it.

As with everything, this will likely be a constant check I keep throughout my life, with the knowledge of my family's history as well as my own. I've learned to take a holistic approach to this simply because I caught it early enough to combat it on my own. Much like I mentioned in my foreword, however, I acknowledge that if it gets out of my control, I do need to seek professional help. I've learned that this isn't the weak solution—this is the proactive, strong, stable solution. To continue improving, I needed to learn how to combat it, and at least for now, I've accomplished that. My goals aren't simply to make it to the next day—my goal is to continue moving forward, to grow into the person I know I can be, and to do this, I needed to address my problems head on. I'm proud of this.

Chapter Three
Holidays and Other Difficult Times

I'm writing this on the eve of Christmas Eve. Christmas Eve Eve. I was just at Walgreens doing some last-minute Christmas shopping. This is normal for me. I procrastinate. All of the empty moving boxes in my apartment can attest to this—I'm moving in two weeks.

And it's said that notoriously the holidays are the most difficult time after you've lost a loved one, but I didn't think this would be true for me, despite what everyone was telling me. However, like most things during the mourning process, this shifted. And even as I began to recognize this shift, I continued to try to convince myself that this time wasn't any more difficult. Even as I began to recognize this shift, I'd still say, "No, holidays aren't that difficult because Jake and I didn't do anything out of the ordinary for them. For us, it was just another time of the year."

And this was true in part—we didn't do anything particularly special. Even though last year I cried in the middle of *A Christmas Carol*, I still said, "Nope, not hard." I justified my tears because I imagined Scrooge was suffering from the same demons Jake had, and I hated to see people judge him in that play. I hated to see the crowd judge his character, too. I flashed back to how cynical Jake had been on his last Fourth of July, which used to be his favorite holiday, and I immediately latched to Scrooge's character as completely misunderstood.

But back to Christmas Eve Eve, back to tonight, at Walgreens. I planned this trip to be a quick in-and-out quest—I knew exactly what I needed to get. I had gotten my aunt a box of sampler tea for her birthday a month ago, and I planned to get her this M&M's mug I saw a week before, as well as a throw blanket that was on sale. A card, too, because she's a sucker for those.

When I got there, the entire store was filled with couples doing last-minute Christmas shopping, talking about what they should get their parents. As I was looking at a Snoopy card I was planning to give to my aunt, I eavesdropped on a couple discussing how they'd address the inevitable "So when are you two getting married?" questions they'd get from both sides of their families. Their reasons were lame, in my opinion, though I can't remember any of them. I found myself wondering what Jake and I would have done. Our reasons, I told myself, would have been far superior, filled with surreal facts and outlandish excuses. I also can't remember any of the reasons I came up with, so it's possible they were equally as lame as the couple I was eavesdropping on.

I never realized how important holidays were for me and Jake until this moment. While we never addressed it, and while we really didn't get into the whole gift-giving thing, it's that communal bond of knowing the other is there. Even when we were cruel to each other, there is something magical about reciprocated love around the holidays. I'm not sure if this is instinctual or not to couple up during the cold months—from an evolutionary standpoint, I guess that would make sense, but I have no facts to back that up.

What happened at the store next is incredibly embarrassing, and while I tried to cover it up, I couldn't. I cried. I cried, hard. Gasps, sobs, heaves, all of it. Right into that Snoopy card (which, don't worry, I bought). Did people notice? Hell yeah, they did. It was hard *not* to notice the girl having a mental breakdown in the middle of the Hallmark aisle on Christmas Eve Eve. Am I still avoiding this Walgreens? Yes. Yes I am. Even though I'm pretty secure in myself, I'm avoiding it like the plague (though it's right around the corner from where I live). Until I'm sure those who were working there have forgotten, I will be sure to go to the much less convenient Walgreens five miles away, or even better, not shop at Walgreens anymore.

And yes, when Jake was alive, we didn't treat holidays as anything special. We were never the couple to get each other elaborate gifts, to snuggle up by the fire listening to only *Frank Sinatra's Greatest Hits* album, to sip cocoa while watching Hallmark movies, as we imagined less superior couples were doing. If we got the other a gift, it was usually somehow, in some way, for both of us—whether it was a book I'd promise to lend him later, or an album we'd listen to later. An investment. If we got cards, it was probably an otherwise blank page, folded in half, saying something akin to, "Yeah, I guess you're okay," and accompanied by a cartoon tied to some inside joke we'd be forced to explain if the wrong relative saw it. A game.

It was difficult to pinpoint what I missed because it wasn't a specific thing—it was a feeling. Amidst the chaos of holidays, these simple moments kept me warm. I've come to learn that when people say holidays are hard, it's because of that feeling, not because of the weight we held on holidays while he was alive. After a person is gone, what seemed mundane at the time leaves the largest hole in your chest because it's easy to feel you took it for granted, now that it's no longer there.

Many of the things I found stressful during the holidays I now miss, even if they were not exactly the most healthy at the time. After two years of dating, he either refused to go to my family's Christmas, or he made sure to make a quick departure. This wasn't because he hated my family, but because his family had so many traditions tied to the holidays that he hated to miss. He loved these traditions, and he didn't want to miss a minute. Because I saw the root of it, that these traditions were important to him, I didn't force it. Despite this, I remember the stress of trying to plan out both holidays with both families—to ensure I was spending enough time with my family and with his, knowing he would never be at mine. For so long, I assumed this was normal—unchanging. Being able to experience a holiday without this for the second time is strange because it begins to become routine. The third time is when it sets in that "this is your new norm," at least for now. Even though I hated this about the holidays—a stress that I acknowledged few had to deal with, but was too timid to address—I missed it, dearly. I even missed the stress. I felt nostalgic when I wasn't having a panic attack planning how to make sure my family didn't feel neglected while still going to his family's events.

(To be clear, this wasn't his fault, and it's something I hid from him. I should have addressed this, rather than holding it in and saying everything was okay.)

Those first and second times are still covered by raw emotions (like me crying at Scrooge last Christmas), and you're still dealing with those emotions on a more minute-by-minute basis. They happen more often when they're raw. And the third time, I'm finding, is no different (like me crying into a Snoopy card). Now, three holidays later, those emotions remain. And it doesn't seem like they will be going away. They're still visceral and real, no matter how much time passes.

***

During end-of-the-year holidays, these emotions are condensed into a two-week period—where you usually don't have work, or work is much slower (at least in my industry). As time passes, families stop asking how you're doing and start asking if you're seeing anyone, and there is the communal rhetoric that, after a certain age, holidays are for couples or sassy aunts who like to remind you that "[they're] not single so long as they have a bottle of Merlot and a Magic Mike movie to watch later that night." This can feel great—a distraction from the pain inside your head—or it can feel incredibly isolating. The memories you hold from your past life linger, the traditions from before fester—and the happiest memories can turn your mood sour knowing they're no more.

As I mentioned, Jake's family was heavy on traditions during the holidays. First, there would be the white elephant gifts with his mom's side of the family, then once her side of the family would leave for the night, there would be the secret Santa we'd play with his immediate family, mostly his younger siblings. I'd go home to get ready for their Midnight Mass, and he and his brothers would pick me up in their dad's Cadillac to go to an old cathedral downtown. This was the same, every year.

My family has never been this heavy on tradition, possibly because we're much smaller. It was easy to dip out of my family's holiday because there was no agenda—no set plan. As stressful as it was to plan out his family's holiday without neglecting my own family, I missed this the first year I didn't have it, and even more the second and third years. For eight years, this was my life, and it was strange the first time it didn't happen—and even stranger the second and third times.

Now, I've found how important it is for me to make traditions—not to replace these memories, but to ensure I'm continuing to make the holidays joyful, to carry over what I've learned to love from this past life and make it my own. This joy is admittedly more constructed and mindful, but as I work through this, I'm learning how to truly appreciate the holidays for what they will be for me going forward.

Two years ago, I started a tradition making a gingerbread house for when my mentally handicapped aunt comes into town for the holidays—an hour spent with just me and her, crafting not only the perfect, avant-garde gingerbread house design, but also the story behind it. Who would live there, what was special about it, who had owned it before, and so on. Again, my family is much smaller than Jake's was, but I'm growing to appreciate this—I'm spending more time picking out presents for each person, meditating on what I appreciate about each person, and thinking of what would be the best present to gift. I've grown to further appreciate my own family now that I'm spending the entire holiday with them—and as an adult, I'm able to truly foster that relationship instead of treating it as simply another task. I've grown to understand what holidays truly are about, especially in a family that isn't truly religious (we have no religious ties to Christmas, no church obligations—simply family time).

I cherish the times spent hanging out in our kitchen, helping my mom make an overly elaborate feast for six, quoting Monty Python and listening to music with my dad, and catching up with my brother and his wife (they live in Cleveland now, so I don't see them as often as I'd like).

Again, as I mentioned before, these nerves from my past life do not numb. They're always raw, and especially around the holidays. What has helped me is to repurpose these events in my life mindfully—to ensure I'm not isolating myself, to spend this time appreciating those who are still with me, and those who have stuck by me throughout everything, and to give them a gift to show them how much I care. The holidays are a wonderful time to do all this. It's still difficult, but spending this downtime during the coldest months to build relationships—not necessarily romantic, but also familial and friend—has helped me better understand what holidays are truly about.

However, no matter how busy I try to make my holidays, it's difficult to avoid the memories lingering from before. The last Christmas Jake and I had together I especially remember, though there wasn't anything special about it—we were both "on." I remember, even though he

15

skipped my family's Christmas, there was something about the way he put his arm around me during their white elephant game, the warmth I felt, the deep connection I felt when I looked in his eyes when we silently plotted on how we'd get the record player that was making its way around the circle. His eyes were clear, connected, unclouded. I've grown to cherish this memory, and I'm happy that this is one of my last holiday memories with him—of him as I knew he was behind that mask.

At times, this makes it more difficult because of the inevitable "what could have been" if he had gotten the help he needed. But I'm learning, slowly but surely, that I can't continue to have these thoughts if I truly want to move forward. I have to learn to accept what happened, to stop retreating in my mind and exploring how I could have fixed what happened.

These traditions I've formed with my family began to build the base, and as I spend more holidays with this as my new "norm," I've learned how to repurpose this difficult time in my head. I'm learning it will always, on some level, be difficult. But by staying mindful, I am learning how to enjoy holidays, despite this hole. This hole is still gaping, open, but I'm mindful of filling it with meaningful experiences with my own family—stable connections and new memories.

Chapter Four
Mindful Rituals

When you've lost everything, it's easy to cling to a self-crafted routine. Because you made it, and you control yourself, this is unchanging, stable. And it's easy to cling to this stability once you've experienced how unstable the world is around you. For me, I found this stability in things like reading every day, making healthy meals for myself, and going for walks—surface-level, positive daily rituals that have helped me grow physically and mentally stronger each day.

After I returned from my trips, I realized I needed to ensure that my base was solid. Was true. Was honest. To do this, I needed to evaluate where I was each day. I decided that, for me, the best way to reset my mind each morning was to go for a walk before work—so every morning at 6:00 am, I go for a walk. This took a while to finally become a routine because above everything, I love my sleep, but with time, I've adjusted, and I feel much better for it. Rain or shine. Sleet or snow. Whether I fall asleep at 2:00 am or 10:00 pm the night before, this is now how I start my day, every day.

While this might work for me, I acknowledge it might not work for everyone. For me, it's the meditative act. Every morning, I walk the same path but with different music. I walk on the rails of the railroad tracks that divide the parking lot from the park, and I try my best to not look at the ground while still keeping my balance. My goal? To look forward the entire time without looking down at my feet—while still looking forward, toward the sunrise. It's a strange thing I started over the summer, and I latched onto it. I like this. At first, I loved the symbolism of it, but now, it's almost a form of meditation. I'm regaining my balance much better than I had, even this summer.

For the most part, I see the same people every morning. We wave to each other, but other than that, we keep to ourselves. Once I get to the park, me and the same three old men wave to each other, without saying a word. We send a simple nod, wave, then walk our separate ways, on the same forked path—and to me, that is an absolutely beautiful thing to experience just as the sun rises, as the cold wind hits my face. I live for these mornings.

Whatever it is you do that works for you—if it's going for a run every morning, doing yoga, writing, having coffee while reading a book—do it. For me, getting my blood rushing first thing in the morning is what keeps me positive and centered. Especially because I work from home, this is a necessity for me. If you start on a positive note, before you dive into the mundane details of the day, you will view everything else in a different light. If you go into a terrible meeting after going on a spectacular walk, this dulls the hurt.

I'm not a doctor—this is what works for me, and it was through trial and error. I tried doing yoga in my apartment and I tried writing in my apartment, but it wasn't until I *left* my apartment every morning and breathed some fresh air right away—an escape from everything I know I need to do and a time to let my mind ease into the day—that I was able to refocus myself on what matters in life, on what makes me happy, and how I can get closer to reaching my goals every day.

Sometimes, this meditation just isn't possible. For example, this morning (which, at the time of writing this, is early January), the latch of my door was stuck in the latch hole, meaning that I was stuck in my apartment. I could not go on my morning walk. I tried to unscrew the handle and the door hinge and everything, but without a power screwdriver (which I really should get), there was no way the screws were budging. I literally could not leave my apartment, which is what I taught myself was the only way to escape my demons. Though this was only a minor setback, I felt I was retreating into my shell. This was the first time in two months I hadn't gone on a morning walk when I knew I was working at home for the rest of the day. Because this just happened, I'm going to try to bring you into the scene that was *this morning*, and I'm going to try to analyze it as best I can afterward.

For science? Here we go:

First, I woke up at 6:00 am. Immediately, to make sure I got out of bed on a good note, I turned on Al Green's "Like a

Ram," as I've been doing for the past two weeks. (I can't get enough of this song.)

I put on my fleece leggings; my favorite flared walking jeans over that; my new Handsome Jack shirt from a show I went to in St. Louis about a month ago (November 24); my Alice Cooper sweater; another plain grey sweater; my good, trusty, pilled-up seven-year-old pea coat; as well as my socks, scarf, hat, and shoes. (Wisconsin weather, *amirite*?)

And as I was about to open the door, I twisted the knob, but the door wouldn't open. I looked at the side view of the door, between the door and doorframe where the latch goes into the latch hole, and I saw that the latch was stuck again. (This had been happening on and off for the past five months, but usually, if I thrust my body against the door, I'm able to open it.) This time, there was no such luck (*my poor neighbors*). I tried to unscrew the door, but I couldn't get the screws to move. I called maintenance, but I know that time wise, they're less than efficient.

Rather than acting rationally, I panicked. I clung to the idea that this was the only way I could start my day on a sane note, though only moments before, I was in a great mood. Immediately, I not only felt trapped in my apartment, but also trapped in my head and in my thoughts, which were spiraling to a worst-case scenario. My hands clenched—the first sign of a panic attack.

And it wasn't even about my safety, of the obvious fire hazard I was facing. It was mostly about missing my walk that day— how I would feel mentally without this cold burst of air in the morning, without the sun or wind hitting my face right away, without stretching my legs before I sat down to work for the day. I feared the worst—and without even thinking of how I could avoid it, I feared the inevitability of regression, as if I had no control over it if I didn't get this walk in. Especially on a Monday, I feared how this would impact the rest of my week, which was carefully and intricately planned to get the most out of every moment outside of work. In my head, I scrapped all plans this week, planning instead for a mental breakdown.

All because I couldn't go for a walk.

This is not sustainable.

While I do think starting the day with a walk is an incredibly healthy habit to get into, when it becomes an obsession, this is when it shifts to unhealthy—kind of like how eating disorders or exercise obsessions develop. When the mind shifts to obsession, a once-healthy focus becomes mentally unhealthy. This balance of mental and physical health is incredibly sensitive—if one begins to trump the other, there's a disparity, which can impact both sides.

For me, I've always had difficulty with this balance, so being mindful of this is incredibly important to me. When I was a kid, I used to be obsessed with thinking I was a chunky kid because at one point in elementary school, someone called me fat. (Looking back on pictures, I was actually pretty skinny, but that's beside the point. Kids suck sometimes, and they're mean to each other before they realize their words actually impact others.)

I clung to the idea that I needed to be skinny like I thought everyone else was, so I would stay up late at night doing sit-ups, squats, and push-ups. My parents had no idea of this because I would make sure they were asleep before going into the basement and turning on MTV as quietly as I could. If they came down, I would pretend like I couldn't sleep and that I was just watching music videos. I would show up to school exhausted, unable to concentrate, unable to connect—all because I was trying to fit what I thought I should be in my head.

Though I was just fine as I was, I didn't question my behavior. I thought this was how I would be a normal, functioning kid, one who wouldn't be bullied anymore. This led to a number of issues down the road with my personal expectations for how I looked, and how I executed my goals. I convinced myself that if I did not do these things every day, I would spiral into a deep, impenetrable pit of gluttony and sloth, and that would be the end of everything for me (spoiler: that's not at all the case). That careful balance between physical and mental health was seriously skewed.

It went beyond what others thought of me. I got it in my head that "this is what I need to do." (I wish I had the foresight to have this same vigor toward something more productive, like learning Mandarin or studying philosophy.)

I realize this is more extreme than walking every morning, but I hope you can see the connection I'm going for—sometimes, rituals can do more harm than good, however healthy they may seem on the surface. I appeared physically healthy and I was eating all of the right foods, but my attitude toward getting there was mentally unhealthy. I'm happy that I was able to snap out of this, and to be honest, Jake was a huge part in challenging these demons head on, simply by challenging their root and questioning why I was doing these things in the first place. I will forever be grateful that he did that for me. But it's easy to forget these lessons as soon as trauma hits. When it does, routines can easily become your life, like my obsessive daily walking routine. Something to fill your head, to cover up those incessant festering thoughts. I could not continue as I was if I wanted to be a functioning member of society if I had such self-induced cinder blocks in my mind.

It's unrealistic to believe I can take a walk every morning without any sort of setback. Inevitably, there will be times where I will not be able to go for a walk, and I should be able to learn how to cope with those times in order to truly feel comfortable within society, as an individual. That's the ultimate goal.

As I mentioned at the beginning of this book, I offer what I've learned, and I present what I'm still working on. This is something I'm still working on, and I think it's something most people suffer with on some level. It's easy to settle into a routine because it's comfortable, and it's difficult to change that routine because any change has the potential to fail. It hasn't been tested. These failures seem to take front row when you're first starting a routine, but as long as they're positive, it's through habitually working at them that you grow past failure. It's difficult to remember that all of your routines were once something new, were once something that could have potentially failed (even something as simple as brushing your teeth or washing your face at night). They became comfortable the more you worked at them. Once a routine grows stale, this process has to start over again (unless we're talking about brushing your teeth—please continue to do this, for all of our sakes). It's never comfortable when it starts, but through each new challenge, you grow stronger. The only way you can continue to grow is if you continue to challenge your routines.

This is one of my goals for this year—to learn to challenge my homeostasis. If anything, it gives the brain a break to explore different ideas rather than those I force through my head, trying to force a stale routine to stay relevant when it no longer is. We often forget to look at what we're doing, and we wonder if there's a more fruitful and fulfilling way to reach our own goals. We also forget to reanalyze our goals, to make sure they truly fit who we are and where we'd like to be—long term, rather than superficial short term.

These hyperfocuses detract from your experience in this world, your ability to explore the world around you, your full journey. Is the world terrifying? Looking at the daily newsfeed, it sure seems like it. But that doesn't mean you should retreat behind a careful set of rules for yourself just because you're too focused on controlling the minutiae.

Should you still be mindful and work toward self-improvement? Absolutely. Improving yourself should be your number-one priority, because ultimately, you should try to be the best version of yourself— no matter where you are in life. But there's no way you can be that best version if you're not mentally present. And you cannot be mentally present if you are constantly trying to construct your life with pieces that no longer fit. Your brain will forever remain scattered.

Especially after experiencing significant loss, it can be easy to cling to a routine. You are in control of your own routine. It is comfortable. It is constant. But if you get too attached to routine, you may not stop to think if it has overstayed its welcome, or if you could benefit from changing it. If anything, to be a dynamic human being, it's important to, at times, challenge yourself and change your routine, to make sure what you are doing is best for yourself while also exposing yourself to a potentially different way to live—even if it's just cutting out coffee in the morning, or maybe cleaning your kitchen in the morning and reading at night.

I was talking with someone recently who said you should never walk the same path twice in one week. While I think this view would be extreme to be applied everywhere, this idea has resonated with me on a more philosophical level. Instead of continuing to do the things you've always done, you should constantly question if what you consider constants are actually helping you in the long run. If maybe there would be a more efficient way to do what you are already doing. If maybe there would be something else you could add to enhance what you already think is a great routine. *Don't fix what isn't broken* is a great philosophy to a point, but that doesn't mean you should give up changing or challenging yourself completely. To progress, you have to work on it, even if it's the smallest things in your life.

CHAPTER FIVE
WHY I WILL NEVER SAY, "I'M BETTER NOW!"

The short answer? Because I really do not want to lie to you. I'm not better—I'm different. It doesn't get easier—it gets different. And this shouldn't be scary, because once I figured this out and accepted it, I've been able to learn which healthy coping methods work best for me.

The long answer? Recently, I started taking only cold showers because, supposedly, it's better for your skin and your lymphatic system. (Also, I just moved, and my water heater is now less than efficient. It seemed to be the natural progression.) I was told by multiple people who have done the same that I will eventually grow to "love it." That I will find it to be "meditative." That my body will "adjust to and accept" this horrifically icy challenge.

Three weeks in, this is not the case. I still dread every cold shower. I do this every other morning, right after my walk, as some sort of sick joke to myself. It is not as refreshing, nor is it as relieving as they promised me. Especially this winter, where my home base of Milwaukee hit a record low of –50°F, it's God-awful. Of *course* I feel more awake because I am literally shocking my body, and all of the blood rushes to the surface of my skin.

Sigh.

Because my blind determination is sometimes my biggest flaw, I'm sticking with this because I told myself I would try it for two months, no matter what. You can choose to have sympathy for me or not. Either way, I'm still going to finish the remaining five weeks, and I will probably complain about it every time it comes up.

I will never say that I like cold showers. Never. I will never like cold showers. However, I've learned methods to get through them, and I'd like to think this made me stronger.

I've learned that I cannot shave my legs in the cold water without shaving cream, especially not with a safety razor (I never used shaving cream, telling everyone much too confidently that "it's just another commercialist construct"), and I've learned that I do in fact need to wash out all of the shampoo from my hair, even if it is painful. Right now, my shower times last one Handsome Jack song—usually "Keep On," but it depends on what I'm feeling. Once it hits the breakdown at the end, I know my suffering is almost over, and I should probably wash all of the soap from my body.

This is a stark contrast from the half-album (usually something from Dr. John or The James Hunter Six) shower karaoke dance session it used to be, but I'm learning how to get through it.

These showers are not getting easier, but I'm learning how to navigate through them so I'm not getting pneumonia. Now, I know what I'm getting myself into, and I know how to get through it as best as I can.

Each time I get in that shower, I'm equally raw, equally numb, and my nerves react exactly as they did that first, fateful January day that I decided to take a cold shower.

I don't mean to diminish the PTSD pain I still suffer, but I hope you can see the parallel I'm trying to draw here.

As with my cold showers, when I wake up in a cold sweat, or when something triggers me in the day-to-day, I know it's going to be rough. There is no building of callouses in this situation. You cannot build callouses around all of your nerves. At least for me, it's always equally raw. While some nerves may dull with time, others will always be equally painful. Sometimes, the nerves that were once dulled will suddenly stab with pain when hit from a different direction.

Since my recent move, I've had to change my walking path. I'm no longer by the park I mentioned in a previous essay (the one with the railroad tracks), so I usually walk around my new neighborhood.

There is now a person who passes me on my walks each day who has Jake's smile. It's not exactly the same—he's older, his voice is different, and he's much friendlier than Jake would have ever been to a passerby (not that Jake wasn't friendly, but this man goes out of his way to say hi, whereas Jake was more of a nod-in-your-direction kinda guy).

What is the same is Jake's squinty-eyed smile, where the blue eyes scrunch under a strong brow. This was the thing that mattered—the smile was where the memories lay because, in my mind, all of the memories I wanted to remember of us together were of those where he was smiling his most authentic smile. *This* smile.

At first, it cut me—in this man's smile, I could hear Jake's voice laughing. I missed being with Jake. I missed his sense of humor. I missed everything. The shock of seeing it repeatedly on another face was enough to make me change walking paths.

Turns out that even though I changed paths, I still pass him, because I'm pretty sure he lives on the same block as me and we live in a grid. I couldn't hide from it, no matter how hard I tried. I had to learn how to cope. I had to learn to cope with him making small talk as we inevitably realized we were both walking every day—as we built an unspoken camaraderie based on similar habits. Even now, almost a month later, this nerve is raw whenever I see him smile. But I've learned how to cope with it in my head and to smile back and ask him about his day. This goes beyond the simple act of acknowledging this person. I had to learn to interact with *society* again—to attempt to change the context, day by day, walk by walk, instead of hiding from something I would inevitably encounter again.

This is good. It sounds cliché to say, but learning to deal with these ultimate low points has helped me better cope with the lows that everyday life throws at me. The context has been established—I know I can get through it now if I just address it head-on instead of ignoring it.

As I mentioned in my first book, I still have dreams of finding Jake, meshed with surreal, traumatic storylines usually tied to whatever book I'm reading. While they're slowly becoming less frequent, they're still there, and they're still equally painful. I know, now, that as soon as I wake up from this, I need to take care of it at that moment. I need to reflect on myself before I move forward with my day. This doesn't happen every day, and there's no way I can see it coming, unlike the walks where I see Jake's older doppelganger almost every time. It ambushes me, guerilla warfare–style in a place that used to be a safe haven—my dreams. It's not going away, but I've had to learn to work through it in that moment. I've learned that I can't shut it out, not once—I have to work through it every time instead of burying it.

Again, I'm not saying this is easy. It's painful, every time. Burying it would save me the immediate pain I suffer, absolutely. I think that's natural—as humans, we want to avoid pain, mental or physical. But the difference between physical pain is that most of the time, the body can repair itself. Mental pain can only be repaired if you work at it, habitually, with intent and purpose. And sometimes, it seems even more painful to address this head on, when it's fresh—but often, at least from my experiences, this will help you from enduring it for longer. Working through it is a painful, short stab; repressing it is a throbbing, festering wound. The stab will go away, but the throb—it will morph into something different, if you continue to ignore it. There can't be a day where you say, "Well, I'm going to push this one back, just for today." Even if it's just one time, it still festers. Your brain cannot fix itself—you have to actively work to fix it, every time.

For me, my mental pain is mostly centered around one specific context, which is the pain I suffer from missing my partner, Jake. But like most things in life, one carries into the others, into ones I would have never expected—like my neighbor's smile.

These guerrilla memories aren't always traumatic. When I see a bag of peach rings, I think of Jake because it was his favorite candy. When I hear Red Fang, I think of Jake because it was his favorite band. When someone does the "Goodbye Horses" dance from *Silence of the Lambs*, I think of how, through months of practice, Jake had perfected that dance much better than anyone really should ever do. Sometimes, these memories make me smile; other times, it takes me back and forces me to sit down and repair myself for a minute. Though they're positive memories, they're equally painful to rehash knowing he isn't here anymore, knowing they're limited to my memories. For example, a few months after Jake had killed himself, I had to leave a comedy open mic to cry in the bathroom because someone tried to do a poor rendition of the "Goodbye Horses" dance on stage, and I *knew* Jake could have done a much better job. When someone asks you why you're crying, *that "Goodbye Horses" dance* is a strange response when out of context.

I'm getting better at this. But does that mean it's getting easier? No. It's difficult every time, but I'm learning how to better cope with it all.

Sometimes, it will never be better, but the goal is homeostasis—staying above water. That is okay. As long as you are doing everything you can possibly do to be better in a healthful way, you are doing a great job, and you are stronger than those who ignore it and hope it disappears. This head-on combat does not get easier—it gets different with each day and each hurdle. This shouldn't be disheartening to you. This should empower you. The only way you know your strength is if you actively work toward improvement and challenge yourself, instead of shut things out. By repressing your pain, you're also repressing your strength. And though I do not know you nearly as well as you know yourself, I know that you can do it not because you're special—but because you're stronger and more capable than you think.

CHAPTER SIX

I BELONG HERE, AND MY ROOTS ARE GROWING

The year following Jake's death, it was difficult for me to find a space where I felt I truly belonged. My brain was scattered, nomadic. Whenever I felt out of place, instead of adjusting, I'd run, hide, or leave. I tried to rebuild, but I didn't give myself the time or the tools to do so. The base I stood on, one I spent most of my life constructing, was chipping away with each trip I took, then reconstructed with cheap plywood. With each regression I made in an attempt to force myself forward, my base grew weaker.

The strong, stable growth I needed was not something I could force. No matter how desperately I wanted it, I could not force myself into recovery. I tried to force what I thought recovery would look like, rather than what recovery actually was for me. It turns out that when you push yourself in the direction you *think* you should be going, rather than where you truly should be, it's hard to stand up straight (especially after a few drinks, as I mentioned in Chapter 2).

When you suppress yourself, be it by holing up or through constant erratic motion, you become your own world, and you become suffocated in that world. Your roots—they stop growing before they can truly be anchored and stable. Much like a maple tree trying to grow in the Sahara Desert, starved, you cannot grow past your own world if you do not nurture those roots.

I'm very fortunate that, despite my stubbornness, I learned this quick enough to put myself on the right path again. This was partly because of my last tour—it was a push in the right direction where I forced myself to analyze my story, discuss my story, share my story. I forced myself to root again, and my story helped me grow as I continued to share it. By sharing openly, by listening to people's insight on my own story and worldview, and listening to their stories and views, my base grew stronger—grew roots. The only way you can better understand someone's world, however dissimilar to yours, is if you interact with it honestly and openly. Not everyone will accept it, and while that's okay, you should always be kind and try to see their point of view, even if you don't agree with it. It's in this cordial dissent that we grow stronger, together. If anything, maybe it will help you gain a different perspective.

The bravest thing you can do is to allow yourself to be vulnerable, honest, and true. It's scary. There are so many people in the world who seem to have it all together, when in reality, nobody does. The perfectly cultivated lives we craft for Instagram and other social media platforms—they're only snapshots of an otherwise normal life. Even if you're Kylie Jenner, you still have to take out the trash once in a while (I'm guessing—I don't know her personally). I'm guilty of this, too, simply because it seems logical that nobody wants to see the average parts of your life. You post the exciting things because you're excited about them, too, and you want to share them with others. This is no different than those you are comparing yourself to.

Everyone struggles, even if it's in a way that is completely foreign to you. That unshakable base of wanting to connect with those around us is the same—even if someone's story differs from yours, we all connect in that we all have struggled, and we are all trying to navigate this complex world. These deep, meaningful connections often happen in the minutiae, the vulnerabilities—not because of the pictures you post from your trip to Belize.

My favorite bit of philosophy is from Michel de Montaigne, who said, "Kings and philosophers shit—and so do ladies." Even though we don't see it (hopefully, at least), everyone has this vulnerability in common. From Mahatma Gandhi to Martin Luther King Jr. to Neil Peart from Rush, my personal idol, those who preceded us shat and those who we hold on high pedestals now still shit. We all have this in common. If we all share one common ground, it is that we all shit.

It's not pretty, but it's authentic, it's honest, and it's probably the most vulnerable thing we all do every day.

(Or every other day. No judgment.)

I don't mean this negatively. I hope that this resonates in that I want us to accept our vulnerabilities—to own our weaknesses as strengths, or at least as something that makes us truly human. By discussing these weaknesses, we process them as they grow outside of our minds. Instead of ignoring them and letting them fester, instead of hiding them behind façades of strength, to share our true selves with others is to become more comfortable in even our most vulnerable weaknesses. In this review, in this openness and honesty, we can find strength in even our weakest moments.

For as long as I can remember, I've struggled with telling my honest, true story. This was half of my battle with the last book—I couldn't write an embellished version of the truth. I'm proud to say that I think I accomplished sharing my honesty and truth with you, as best as I could.

To me, it always seemed much more appealing to tell a story much better than my own—to mechanize a version of myself that I thought would be much better accepted by those around me.

These deviations gave me so much more anxiety than I already had. Instead of comfortably sharing my own story, I would house it on a cubic zirconia platform and try to pass it off as diamond. When I realized it didn't fit, I would often panic, which came off as manic, which often came off as crazy and disconnected with the world around me because I would fabricate it. There was no way I could be a genuine human being this way. If we're going to go back to the Montaigne passage, you could say I was emotionally constipated.

I'm fortunate that, for the most part, I've grown out of this, and I have a great group of friends who check me when it comes back, though it's been coming back less and less as I get older, as I learn to accept my true self and be proud of my own life's story. It wasn't until I started being wholly honest that I realized my story is worth telling. And I realized that this story was much less stressful to maintain compared to the tangled web of messy stories I had fabricated.

Especially as a natural storyteller, I loved the idea of a good story, and because I didn't own my own story, I would simply adopt a new one. But as any good storyteller knows, a good story has to have a base. I did not have that. And the best story you can tell is a true story, one that is rooted in honesty, even in fiction. If the protagonist isn't rooted in at least a little truth, if the character is constantly hiding his or her vulnerabilities, the reader cannot make a connection. And for yourself, if you're crafting your own story, you cannot challenge a crafted persona on any sort of higher level. Your character can only go so far.

What have I learned from this? I've learned that I think my actual, vulnerable self is pretty kickass. I'm stronger than I gave myself credit for, and I'm a lot smarter than I gave myself credit for.

I learned, through being open and honest, that the honest and true stories *are* the most interesting—they're filled with vulnerabilities and awkward moments, and they're *yours*. It's easy to think that you're boring because you live in your head every day. You live with yourself and your thoughts, and you know yourself better than anyone else ever will. But nobody else can hear those thoughts, or see your inner fears. By opening up about these honestly, this will (hopefully, sometimes) give them perspective. Even if it doesn't, in the end, it is much less stressful for you. You can leave that interaction with some sense of absolution—a "Well, that didn't work out" versus "Oh, that mask really didn't go over well. Which mask should I wear next?"

Even if your goal was to only cover up your weaknesses, by doing so, you also cover up strengths that you didn't even know you had.

Once I was able open up about who I truly am, I noticed that I'm much more creative, and it's so much easier to accomplish the things I actually want to accomplish. It's easier for me to create something that I'm 100% behind because I'm not trying to make it into something it's not—I put my honest, true voice behind it. Even if it isn't well received, I'm proud of it because I know it's *me*. And if it is received well? Even better, because that means people like me for me, rather than the false voice I was parroting. Because less of my energy is focused on building a persona, on hiding my vulnerabilities, I've found that I really love living in this world. I love living it as who I am today, and I look forward to continuing to explore who I am and continuing to challenge myself to be a stable, more honest, more true version of myself. I hope that this resonates with those I meet, and if it doesn't, I honestly know that maybe this person is someone I shouldn't force a relationship with.

However, back to Montaigne's statement, "Kings and philosophers shit—and so do ladies," even though we all take a deuce now and then, it's important to be mindful of those around you. You can't take a shit in the middle of the party and expect everyone to be totally cool with it. Metaphorically, this is no different than shouting your vulnerabilities to or at others, unsolicited. This is something I also had to learn the hard way—when I would go to a bar, order a gin and tonic, and say "this is for my dead boyfriend, Jake," there was no context established. There was no base for people to work off of, and if anything, you'd probably attract all of the wrong people if you continued to do this.

If you read my first book, I had a very raw chapter about my experience in Iowa City, near the end. I was just learning how to open up about what had happened to me, but I was struggling. I had broken down those walls, but because I was without a map, without navigation through the world outside my mind, I shouted out my problems to everyone—to strangers, to those whom I didn't know, not even their first names. In a manic panic, I exposed myself, and after I realized what I had done, I retreated back into my mind.

I am not saying you should completely filter yourself, but you should be mindful of those around you while still being authentic to yourself. It is not authentic to shout your problems at people without stopping to listen to what they have to say. One is manic, one is mindful. I think you know which is which—I'm sure I don't have to spell this out for you because you're probably much smarter than me.

Moving forward and sharing yourself is a give-and-take experience. There's a reason it's called *sharing*, not thrusting your problems onto someone else. There's a stark difference. Instead of stopping to listen to those around me, in the past, I simply kept going—I've found I'm less mindful about sharing when I don't care for myself, when my base is shaky because I'm not sleeping enough, when I'm working too hard, or when I'm not letting myself process my own internal thoughts before I let them out.

The purpose of exposing your vulnerabilities is to truly connect with someone, which is difficult if you do not give them an opportunity to share their own stories. This pitting of life stories—this is how you learn more about the world around you. This is how you expand your world. This is how you strengthen your own beliefs.

While I was in inpatient the week after I found Jake, there was a psychiatrist I was assigned to during this time, for one-on-one sessions. I was grateful for her in that she was one of the few who respected that I did not want to take medication, and she was incredibly insightful despite never experiencing something like what I had. What she said transcended individual events, and is something I try to keep in mind as I continue to move forward. I'm sure it's something all of you have heard at some point, but she told me that a stable life is a three-legged stool. Each leg has to be equally balanced for it to be stable. One leg is physical health and basic needs are met, one leg is a sense of purpose, and one leg is an emotional support system. If any of these fall by the wayside, the stool will tip over.

And this makes sense. As organic human beings, these three legs are our sustenance. A plant cannot grow its roots without sunlight, without water, without nourishment. No matter how much sunlight and nourishment a plant has, if it doesn't get water, it will die.

Through these three legs—physical health, purpose, and support system—these are your source of sustenance, what makes your roots grow deeper. This should not be suffocating, and this does not mean that you are set in your place forever. Your roots are simply attached to your base, and your base can be mobile. The more your roots grow into that, the stronger your foundation will be. While I spent so much time fearing these roots, suppressing their growth, I was slipping on ice. These roots died as soon as they started to form, and this was by design. I was scared to root down to anything because I had crafted in my mind that "this is how you get old quick." But that's not true. You get old quick by letting your problems consume you—and that doesn't age well.

While my roots are not fully formed, they're grounded. They're stable, and they're growing deeper. And that allows me to stand taller. Even when I am having my roughest days, they are not nearly as rough knowing I have solidity beneath me. The darkness is made much brighter when you have something to catch your fall—whether it is a support system, physical health, or a sense of purpose. And none of these need to be grandiose. They just have to be there, and you have to focus on growing them every day.

These do not appear magically—you have to build these yourself, and with great intention. I am happy to say that now, I feel like I do belong. And I can confidently say "thou must grow roots," but this is something that I continue to be mindful on. A constant check. My focus.

CHAPTER SEVEN
MUSIC AND HEALING

If you read my first book, you'll know that music was truly what taught me how to enter society again. I'm not unique in this. Since the beginning of time, music has been a unifying force—when there aren't words to explain how we are feeling, music seems to fill the place and connect people from completely different walks of life. We can trace the history and migration patterns of our early ancestors through the different musical and artistic trends they left behind, from past to present.

Before writing this chapter, I meant to read a book on one example of how music is impacted by migration (*Chicago Blues: The City & Its Music*—it looks really great), but I never got around to it. Maybe this will be better—maybe then this will be 100% from my heart, instead of from a book I've been neglecting since I purchased it two years ago.

At its core, music binds us together. Chicago blues with Delta influences. New Orleans jazz with Creole influences. Eastern instruments integrating into psychedelic rock as those philosophies integrated with our society. Even if it's just a killer guitar riff or an amazing harmonica solo or even playing spoons and stomping to a beat around a campfire, these sounds unify us—they tug our hearts out of our chests and sew them carefully onto our sleeves.

It's a natural human thing—we want to connect, we want to be a community, and music is our unifying language. It is a powerful, portable force that, no matter where you are from, hits the complete emotional spectrum without speaking a word. That is the most beautiful thing about music—you don't have to say anything. When there's a song on that resonates, you know it, and it resonates with those who know it, too. That common ground is already established before either of you say a word. You just have to nod to the beat and thumbs-up the person next to you. *Bam*—you're friends for that moment. You learn something about that person by the way the person processes the song, by how you process the song.

I was raised in a musical household. For as long as I can remember, I've had a violin in my hand. My mother plays piano and my father plays guitar. One of my first memories is singing "Nowhere Man" as my father accompanied with his guitar, the music laid out in a huge Beatles anthology that I treated as my Bible growing up, even before I could fully read music and understand time and key signatures. I remember feeling the hardships of "Nowhere Man" far before my young world was able to connect with the protagonist's hardships, simply through the way the music made me feel.

In my memory of this moment, it doesn't feel like I had been singing it for the first time, so I'm assuming this is something that I asked for specifically, repeatedly, as a child. This was the first song I can remember actually connecting with—a song that taught me there was a world outside of my little six-year-old sheltered life. Looking back on it, I cannot help but think of how I felt within this memory.

A bit later, in grade school and middle school, I played violin with others at old folks' homes and funerals. Many of my first social lessons—they were through music. You do not play over someone; you play with someone. You follow the same beat, and you agree on a key. If someone openly criticizes you from the audience as you play, you keep playing and try to make it better while staying true to the song's integrity as best you can. You cannot stop and leave—you have to keep playing until the song is done (old folks' homes are brutal— to be clear, this never happened at any funeral I played at). This also taught me an important lesson that I didn't internalize until recently— as I've mentioned before, you cannot connect with everyone, even if you're speaking the universal language of music. But that unifier—it transcends culture or language or past experiences.

When I was in high school, I branched out to chamber and symphonic orchestra. The bond you have with your stand partner is usually tied to the music you play—your bows have to move in sync, you have to agree on who is best suited to flip the page, and, even on a minor level, you have to make sure you're spaced apart enough to not bump into your partner while still sitting close enough to look like a unit. The feeling you have when the entire orchestra nails a song is euphoric. The feeling you have when you notice your bow is the only one moving out of sync, or when your flat note resonates over the otherwise perfect harmony, is the ultimate low. Your individual instrument's voice is unique, and it adds to the dynamic, overall sound, for better or for worse.

If your orchestra is good, you don't care who gets the solo—you're proud for the person who achieved that, and you back that person up with as much energy as was put into the solo (or, if the person flubs it up, you play around the solo—you go with it, because everyone works harmoniously together).

Though it would be a lie to say I lived a hard life growing up (I lived a very fortunate life that I'm incredibly grateful for), music made those typical teenage-angst years much more bearable knowing that artists like Janis Joplin had encountered something similar to what I was feeling at that time, even if only in feeling, and they were able to make something out of it. It made it easier knowing I would be able to put these feelings into Vivaldi's "The Four Seasons"—and that I would be able to process it in every crescendo, every decrescendo, every rest, in a way that words just couldn't do.

My favorite music, the music that resonates with me the most, drove me to write my first book. While writing my first book, I thought, *Okay, now what do I do with this pain, and how can I make it resonate with others?* This teamwork I found through playing with others— this taught me how important it is to rely on others to create a truly dynamic piece, whether it's finding an awesome editor or an awesome friend who agrees to read that piece with honest feedback.

For me, I've always struggled with social anxiety, which may come as a surprise to some because I've covered this up with multiple masks, as I mentioned before. And though it seems like a contradiction, I'm actually naturally a social person, so this anxiety stabbed me every time I tried to do what I wanted to do—to talk with people, to connect with people.

What music taught me is that sometimes, the silences are the most powerful answers, the ones that hold the most weight. The thoughtful pause that is found in rests or in between songs. And what blues taught me is that sometimes, the best response you can give to someone is, "Man, that's rough. I'm sorry to hear that." That feeling the blues gives—that shared pain—creates a base community, a place for your pain to sit and grow into something else (hopefully more beautiful than it once was, if you treat it right and you care for it).

On the other side of the spectrum, Monty Python's Eric Idle wrote the song, "Always Look On The Bright Side Of Life," which was sung at the end of *Life of Brian*, where his character was trying to cheer up those who were being crucified around him as he was hanging from a cross himself. This, while not traditional blues, holds that same integrity, even though it's completely different. The beauty of it is that I can't explain why I feel that way, I just *know* it. You may not agree with me, but that's okay. The way I view the world is shaped by my relationship with music—it was essentially a third parent to me. It helped me grow into who I am today.

This is why during my trips in 2017, I ran after music. For Jake and me, music was also our language. We learned more about each other in the earliest days of dating by exchanging albums back and forth, by watching music documentaries, by going to concerts. For me, music had always been my home, and by sharing music with him, this meant I was letting him into my home. I believe he did the same with me. I remember how incredibly moved I was when he finally invited me to his family's annual Fourth of July celebration, which involved blasting music across the lake his family lived on, finished off by sitting around a fire listening only to Pink Floyd, with casual conversation flowing over the music as if in harmony. This is what he lived for, and I knew something was wrong when he said he didn't love it anymore.

We built common interests through the bands we learned about together and through the shows we went to, and these experiences led us to visit places we had never gone before, in venues we had never known existed. They built a shared philosophy on how we should interact in society, even if this philosophy was based on a Red Fang concert. You treat people with respect, you work with the group, you stand up for people when they are being mistreated. You saw all of this there.

Even in this small microcosm, this taught me much more than I realized at the time. This was similar to my experience with orchestra—it's difficult to put into words the bond you feel with those you play music with, just as it's difficult to put into words the bond you feel when you share music with someone. You have to come together as individuals to truly make a dynamic experience—whether it's in the mosh pit or in playing Handel's *Messiah* in a concert hall.

Especially for him, past the times I went to concerts with him, his family worked in music production. I remember he once told me that he feared he would get bored of concerts as he worked longer in the industry. To my knowledge, this never happened, and I guess that can be the one silver lining out of all of this. Until his final breaths, he still loved the shit out of a great live show. I will not try to dissect why, because that's unfair, and he's not here to speak on that. I'm learning more and more that while I did know him, there were parts of him that I will never fully know, and I'm coming to terms with that.

But for me, music has always been my safe space. It's where I knew I wouldn't be expected to speak, but I knew I would still be able to feel the community around me. The spotlight—it wasn't on me. I could be a fly on the wall and still feel like I was a part of the experience, and that experience would be personal and pitted against my own ones. The person next to me—I can tell if they're feeling it, too. We wouldn't have to say it—we would just have to exchange eye contact, as our implied *hell yeah*.

During a time when I didn't know what was happening, music became my base, my motivation that I could make something out of this hurt—that I could move forward, that I could progress. During a time when I couldn't put my hurt into words, music did that for me. *Honest* music. I was lucky that the bands I followed were honest musicians, but again, this is a chicken or the egg thing (because I'm not sure I would have followed musicians who weren't honest).

Had I been in a slightly better place, I think I would have processed this better. I'm fortunate that I can process it a little better now. Right now, I'm grateful for Chico Hamilton's *Nomad* album, which is blasting through the speakers as I'm typing this. Even though the person sitting on my couch right now is calling it "elevator music," it makes me happy. And right now, despite the shade my couch companion is throwing at it, I'm grateful for every single note Chico is playing.

Chapter Eight
Loving After Losing

I do not have a ready answer to this, so I'm hoping that writing this chapter will help me find some sort of answer in my head, or at least the beginning of one. Right now, a little more than two years after Jake passed so suddenly, I still have difficulties truly loving those around me.

I do love my parents, but I acknowledge at one point they will part from this earth. I love my closest friends, but again, I know they, too, will depart eventually. It is not that I don't care about them. I do—deeply, intensely, and I'm incredibly grateful for them—but I acknowledge that there is an expiration date to every relationship, whether it's through a falling out or through more organic means. I try to keep this out of my mind, but even after about 2½ years, this pain is still fresh, and this thought still lingers in the back of my mind.

This fear—this doesn't keep me from loving, but it does build a wall between me and loving someone openly, truly, and wholly. It's difficult to love someone completely with the "well, this person is going to die eventually" thought whispering menacingly to me as I look into someone's eyes. This would be like renovating your kitchen when you know your house is going to be demolished. It would seem pointless. You stop at a point, and you wonder if it's even worth it in the first place.

However, the only way you can truly love someone is if you are vulnerable with this person, and if you share yourself with them honestly and truly. The only way to truly know if someone can fit into your world is if you let them in—by sharing your truest thoughts, your fears, and your dreams. If you only let others near the periphery and never into your internal home, to put it bluntly, your home will always be empty, even if only in a metaphorical sense.

Even before all of this happened, I've had difficulties with this, and I've addressed this in previous essays. This is something I'm working on— on being honest with how I'm feeling, what I'm thinking, and how I'm processing the world around me with those I care for the most. The *only* way you can truly build relationships with people is if you open yourself up fully, but this is difficult when you wonder if they're going to be there the next day. If this manic internal dialogue of *I wonder if they're going to be there the next day* is at the forefront, it's difficult to have any sort of those uneasy, but necessary conversations.

At times, to avoid these conversations, I hid myself, but this is something I'm actively working on. I need to work on addressing this in myself, addressing that I am worthy of love as I am—that I am good enough to be accepted by those around me, that they don't think I'm dumb or boring and that maybe they do want to spend time with me.

This is something I'm actively working on—I cannot continue to keep my emotions stuffed in a suitcase, ready to uproot at the moment of potential departure. I know this. This is not the kind of love that can grow because it's not sustainable, and I think for a while, I crafted it this way. I crafted it so I could pick up and leave, and I guarded myself from loving wholly because I deemed myself unworthy of love. If anything, as I mentioned before, this is how you get *stuck* in your own mind. You have to unlock these doors, you have to unpack your emotions, and you have to be open.

This was amplified when I lost Jake, and I lost his family at the same time. While admittedly I was always guarded around his family, which was of no fault of theirs, I saw how quickly they left (outside of his mom and his brother) and assumed if they could do it that quickly, so could everyone else. I stand by what I said in the first book—I understand it, truly. To them, I will always be tied to his memory. To them, because I did not let them truly get to know me, they knew me as his shadow. Literally. My nickname was *Shadow*.

Because Jake's personality was so amplified, I stand by that this probably would have happened to anyone he dated. He had a tendency to command the attention of the room—not intentionally, but simply because he was just that witty and charming. Just by being there and being himself, he became the center of the room. But especially since I didn't let my guard down, I never let them truly know me. For me, this *unknowing* was amplified simply by the walls I constructed.

But that aside, I went from seeing them at least once a month for some sort of birthday celebration to not seeing them at all, and knowing this was by design. With each Jake memorial I saw them post online, I knew I was left out intentionally. I know that at least one member of his family blames me for his death completely. Again, I want to address this makes sense to me as much as it can without agreeing with it, but I also want to address that I am human and that this hurt me.

It hurts to be rejected so suddenly, especially after knowing someone for so long. I also acknowledge that, no matter how much I'd like to, there's no way I can change this.

But it wasn't for lack of trying.

For a while, I forced myself to try to connect with his family again, to fit myself into a place I no longer fit. I remember specifically, two weeks after Jake's funeral, I pulled over on the side of a busy road to send someone in his family, someone I knew blamed me completely, a long message. I told him how great of a person Jake was, how great he was to me, and how terrible of a person I am.

I thought this self-deprecation would make him feel better, and maybe it did. I never got a response, so I will never know, and all of that is okay. That's his decision, and he has never been cruel to me, so it's okay. This is how he chose to move on, and what I've said previously is true—I do not hate him for that, I understand that, and I try not to dwell on that. And as I said before, you can't connect with everyone, and you can't make everyone happy without completely losing yourself.

This unsolicited proclamation of self-blame—I thought this would make them feel better, and I thought it would repair the relationship. But it only made me feel worse, and it gave what I truly believe is a false answer. I didn't believe it when I first said it—but I truly wanted them to have a place to put their blame, and I thought I would be able to give that as my parting gift to them, as the answer and the peace that they needed. But the more I said this, the more I internalized it, no matter how much I dwelled on it. It's possible that giving them a scapegoat gave them some immediate comfort, but again, I will never know. This was forced love—real love would have been honest, but because I was frantic, I tried to force them to accept me by knocking myself down to a place I knew I didn't belong.

I know this is common, that the family of the person you lost will either slowly or immediately try to lose contact. I understand the root of it, which keeps it from being in the center of my mind. I get it, but sometimes, this understanding brings the pain internal, rather than at an external scapegoat. A sustained, longing painful, rather than a simple stab of angry pain. Neither is more or less painful—it's just different. Sometimes I wish I hated them because maybe it'd be easier to be on one clear side of the spectrum. But I'm grateful that I do not hate them. I'm grateful that I still harbor positive memories with all of them. Though I do not harbor hatred, this does not heal the hurt of missing the people I grew to know through years of knowing Jake.

Now, I try to make a point to remember only the good times with his family. Much like the positive journaling I mentioned in previous essays, by only remembering good times, it is to cast this relationship in a new light. This light is not false, but true to a specific point in time—because this time together, despite our falling out, is still true, still real. To be hateful for this is to ignore the good times we had, and to unnecessarily bring myself down to a weaker, more hate-filled level. You have to try to look at them as Polaroids close to your heart—and these memories only change if you cast them into the shadows, knowing what you know now. You are in control of this, no matter how difficult it may be. You cannot force them to love you again, but also, they cannot force you to forget these positive memories, or to cast them into negative light. Only you can reshape these memories, and you have control over that, no matter how difficult it may seem.

And while I wish I could convince them to accept me again, I've had to learn that this is no longer possible. This relationship will forever be different, but that doesn't make the past any more or less authentic than how I remember it.

Again, this book is not filled with answers—it is filled with things I am actively addressing and working on. I hope you are able to take something through me stating what I feel, even if it's not exactly the same.

For me, it helps when someone says how they are feeling if I can relate to it, learn from it—and I hope I've done the same for you.

Past his family, I had to learn to move on from Jake. At first, I harbored widowers guilt—the feeling that moving on from him is an assault to his memory. Every relationship seemed temporary to me because, in my mind, I cast him as my one true love, one that nobody else could aspire to. I forgot his flaws and held him on a pedestal. I saw others' flaws more readily because I was comparing them to this godlike figure I had constructed in my mind. I found myself dating people who didn't quite fit me simply because I didn't see a future with them—my mind was still locked on a future with Jake, no matter how impractical I acknowledged that was in my logical mind. I was wasting both of our time simply because I wasn't fully present.

This seems like the most natural place to apologize to everyone I've dated or tried to date in the past 2½ years, because I acknowledge I have not been the most present or the most open. To be clear, while I'm apologizing, this does not mean I think we should get back together, but I simply want to say I'm sorry.

Now that I've gotten that off my plate, I'll continue. Even as I was actively dating, I felt that dating someone new was an assault to Jake. That by loving someone new, I was staining his legacy and forgetting about him completely.

But this isn't true, and I acknowledge that this isn't true. If there is such thing as an afterlife, I am certain that Jake would want me find happiness because I know absolutely that he cared about me more than anyone I knew at the time, and that when he was in his right mind, he would want me to be happy.

But this didn't shake the feeling in my head.

It's difficult to remember this when I'm even *thinking* about building a future with someone else, knowing that he is incapable of doing the same thing. (Unless there's an afterlife. I have no idea. If there is, I hope he's finally dating those hypothetical Swedish twins he always talked about, and I hope they are just as witty and intelligent as he was—and if there is an afterlife, still is.) But, while it may sound a bit callous to say, he's not here anymore, and I still am. If I want to truly move forward, I have to fully move forward. If I find someone to share this life with, awesome. And if I don't, that's okay, too, as long as it feels right to me. But not finding someone because I'm clinging to someone who has passed, because I'm too scared to fully move on—I will have no room to grow if I hold this in my heart.

For the most part, I've progressed past this. I cannot give a reason why—it happened so slowly, over the course of two years, naturally. As I started growing closer to other people, truly, Jake began to hold a different place in my heart. While he will always be there, I've been able to build more stable relationships without completely blocking his memory from my head. In these stable relationships, I feel I am actually honoring Jake—moving in the positive direction I know he'd want me to be.

I'm guessing it's not ideal for those I date, but I try to be honest about it. I've found that, by being honest about it, I learn whether this person truly is a good fit for me. It will forever be a part of me, so I've found it's best to be open about my past and address it as soon as possible in any relationship, as soon as it begins to get serious. It's difficult, and sometimes, relationships that seemed solid will suddenly evaporate, but it's better to know sooner rather than later.

Now, as I'm typing this, I've entered a new stage—the fear of losing the person you've grown to love again.

I believe there are limitless stages of love that I hope to experience with someone again one day. I do honestly believe I experienced these with Jake in our earlier years because we knew each other so well. I can truly say he was my best friend, even later, when we did not treat each other as we should have.

In our earlier years, we had true, honest, pure love. I am certain that I can find this with someone else, and while I know it won't be exactly the same, that's okay. I hope it will be equally as beautiful and as meaningful, and I know this is possible if I truly let it happen.

But it's letting myself be vulnerable enough for it to happen again.

When I seriously tried dating again, I carried a selfish love in my heart—I wanted someone there, and I wanted to make sure I wasn't alone.

Desperately, I fought to make sure I wasn't as alone as I felt, and I thought the only way this could happen is if I locked down a person to stay with. But once you truly connect with someone past surface interests, once you begin to share experiences and build memories together, feeling attached to this person is inevitable. This person becomes your *other*—your best friend, even if only for a while. Once I started to actually feel attached to and reliant upon this person, and once I began to plan even the shadow of a future, I immediately turned my mind to the potential of losing this person.

And I would run.

I knew I wasn't in a place to experience this loss again—I put my present self in a distant future, and that terrified me.

I often tell Petrina (you may remember her—my incredibly patient friend from the first book) that I want to date someone far younger than me because I'm scared to lose someone I love so intimately again like this. While usually I tell her this in jest, this is honest. I am truly fearful of another lover passing on before me, leaving me. I'm truly scared of being alone. Not that it's important to you as a reader, but I usually go for someone a few years older than me. For whatever reason, this seems to work the best for me. Knowing this, even thinking that I would date someone much younger than me shows where my head is at. "I cannot let this person die before me." This love—this love is a selfish love. Dating someone younger for reasons like this is no way to enter a relationship. I realize this.

I know I'm not ready for this pain yet, or even the anticipation of this pain, of looking into the eyes of the person I love the most knowing that one of us will die before the other.

I know I shouldn't think of this—I shouldn't avoid what will naturally happen to all of us. It's a part of the human condition. I should focus on the present, on finding someone who, if it does happen, will make even this most intense pain duller because I will have our memories to keep me company. I hope this person will show me another world I would have otherwise never experienced, and we will grow a world together that, even if this person passes before me, will still feel comfortable and warm to me.

The moments we will share will make it all worth it—and I know this because I often revisit memories with Jake with a fond heart. I know he made me a better person in the end. I am grateful for these memories, and there is no way in hell I would take any of them back, even knowing that it would eventually turn sour, and that he would eventually leave for good.

The reality is we are all here for a finite period of time. I am not immortal, nor you, nor anybody. This fear of death is like fearing a thunderstorm. At some point, it will happen. But that doesn't mean I should carry an umbrella and wear a raincoat on a perfectly sunny, summer day. I cannot retreat from sunshine because of the potential for rain. This fear—this is no way to live. Yes, we should be mindful of it, but it should not detract from the beauty in the beautiful moments. If anything, this inevitability should motivate us to make the most out of every moment—to breathe in the beautiful moments, to build upon these memories shared with the people we love the most. While I have not forgotten this pain, I should learn to move forward from it—to let others in, romantic or platonic, above all else.

I'm working on this.

CHAPTER NINE
FLOWERING FROM THE ASHES

After experiencing significant loss, it can be easy to lose the will to enter the world again. For me, I was incredibly fragile, as I think anyone would be in this situation. When you're in this state, it's easy to retreat because that's what's comfortable to do. And that's okay to do, at first. There is a reason we do this instinctually. We need to give ourselves that time to cry, to mourn, to sleep, to rest. This is for the same reason deer retreat into their safe space in the woods after they've been injured — to heal and mend in a place they know is safe, unchanging.

At first, you *do* need to repair yourself. As long as you're able to do it healthfully, I think this retreat can, to a point, really help. Having days where you don't leave the house is okay, as long as you learn how to cope through these times. I think that's an incredibly powerful skill to have—to learn to manage on your own, in your own space.

It's also an important skill to know when you should ask for help, and when to know it is time to reenter the world. It's important to know when you are able to take care of something yourself, but it's just as important as recognizing when you need to ask for help. Soon, I hope asking for help will be just as easy as retreating when I need to. I'm still working on this, but I hope to get to a point where it comes naturally, where I don't feel like a burden asking for help when I truly need it. And, I can tell you from personal experience that usually, once you open up, people *want* to help.

For me, while I was at my lowest, my worst traits reared their heads and made their presence known—it was by lying, by my inability to set boundaries for myself, by retreating behind a persona to protect myself from my own self-constructed demons. While this was exacerbated by trauma, these unhealthy coping mechanisms were brought in from my past life—things I never addressed even before any of this happened, before I had been able to hide them. Now, they were impossible to ignore.

Trauma does that—at least for me, it pulled my worst traits to center stage.

At first, these traits were the fuel for my manic quest for reason—and I tried to hide them through constant motion. But once I stopped moving and I still saw them there, it made it easier to identify. Instead of allowing these flaws to simmer in the background, where they had been before, I'm fortunate that I kept them in the front, and I began to combat them. This is an ongoing process, as I have to backtrack, find their roots (mostly insecurity), and address deep below the surface. What doesn't kill you makes you stronger, but that only happens if you actually work on getting stronger. Unfortunately, you can't build a six-pack without working on it, no matter how nice that would be.

For Personal or External Reasons—An Argument for Both

Improving for Yourself

At first, I tried to be the best version of myself, so I tried to continue applying advice that Jake had given me as I was before to who I grew into now—as if he was still here giving me that same advice. This created a glass ceiling for my recovery. As much as I would still love to hear advice from him, no matter how otherworldly and eerie that would be, I know I can't.

Despite knowing that this advice no longer applied to my new life logically, I clung to this emotionally. As I grew, Jake's advice did not. I clung to who I was with him, and to the advice he gave me at that time, as a way to preserve his memory. An example of this would be one he showed me through his actions—he was an incredibly motivated, incredibly strong-willed person. And at a certain point in my life, this was good for me because it motivated me to give my 100%, to preserve his legacy. However, this need to give 100% all the time drove me to obsessively chase an unobtainable goal of total perfection, which, if he was here now, I'm sure he would have checked me on. But he's not here anymore to do that, so I took his example and drove it to the extreme—a "this is what he would have wanted me to do."

I had to learn to see his advice as fallible, not all-encompassing. This can be difficult after a person passes, because for whatever reason (even if you're mindful of it), it's easy to put the person on an infallible pedestal, if anything, to maintain his or her memory in your mind. It's easy to forget that the person who passed was also human.

While a lot of his advice was great, and while some of it is still very applicable, I realize now that I had to start rebuilding past the advice he gave me. This was a difficult hurdle for me to jump over—addressing that he is no longer here, and that I have grown past the person I was with him.

As I began to work on what I knew were problems when Jake was alive (mostly because he called me out on it constantly, which again, I stand by—this was a good, selfless thing, and you should always challenge your partner), I began to work toward self-improvement. It is still in the back of my mind that I need to improve for Jake, but now, it's also a daily practice for me, past his memory. I had to address that he is no longer here, and I still am.

I've found that keeping a daily journal helps, if only to force myself to reflect on my day. Writing helps assess how I'm truly feeling, and how I can improve, and it helps me touch on what I've done well that day. It is a mindful meditation, an internal checkup to make sure I'm living as I know I should be—for myself and for others. I try to keep it as positive as possible. For me, self-deprecation was a mask I used to justify my faults, but I've noticed that once I'm more positive about myself, goals seem much easier to accomplish. I check myself more naturally when I acknowledge the things I'm doing right because I'm encouraging them—when I spend more time focusing on what I'm doing right, what I'm doing wrong tends to take a back seat, and honestly, tends to happen less often. When I'm focusing on what I'm doing wrong, it perpetuates the cycle by bringing me down to an unnecessarily low level. I've learned that, for me, when I'm positive, I encourage myself to *continue* living more positively. With it, I truly believe that when I carry confidence, I can achieve anything.

While often I still go back to Jake's advice, I do not hold it as my Ten Commandments, as I had before. They are simply, now, memories of his philosophies that I can still tie into my own life—not chains I should hold myself to. I see them, now, as dynamic, rather than laws to uphold to maintain his legacy.

These were all things I knew I needed to do, for me, for my happiness, for my well-being.

Telling Your Story

We are naturally communal, so to care about your total well-being, it's also important to think of how your actions impact who you respect most. That outside view—this is the most valuable thing we have as humans. If the people sharing their views with you care about you, they will want to see you at peace with yourself, and they will let you know when they're worried. They will be there for you when you need them, when they are able to be present; you should do the same. This is a give and take, a balance that, when you find the right people, should happen naturally. These communities we build as we grow older—they're important. To truly be present in this world, you have to interact with it, past your own personal perspective.

To everyone who truly knows you, they can see these deviations much more readily than you can—they're looking right at you, and they don't have the clutter of inner thoughts that you have in your brain every day. They see the portrait of you at that point, and they are able to associate it with a photo book of memories past—easily comparable to them. (Much like how you notice how long someone's hair has grown after you haven't seen them in six months.) They are able to detect the subtle changes that build over time that you may not be able to realize. Through the tunnel vision of trying to make sure everyone thought I was okay, I neglected everything else that mattered. I canceled plans. I forgot about plans. My jokes turned from natural to manic, which was far more obvious to those I truly knew than I previously realized. I like to think I'm a pretty funny lady, but only when I'm being truly honest with myself—and much like nearly everything else in life, if it's forced or untrue, it's never as good as the real stuff. People let me know, but I chose to ignore them. I justified that they didn't truly know me, but I

56

didn't realize that they *did* know me, outside of my internal thoughts. It's a different kind of knowing, and it's no more or less authentic than your own self-image.

It wasn't until I started truly interacting with people again, wholly and honestly, that I was able to escape my head. Once I started listening to advice, truly talking with others, I felt less lonely. It was easier to motivate myself to rebuild.

While writing my first book, I struggled with thinking, "Why am I sharing this story? Why would anyone care?" Most of my early drafts were ditched not because I thought they sucked, but mostly because I felt that telling my story would be a worthless endeavor—another memoir in a growing pile of memoirs that hit the shelves every day. I assumed that my life was boring, that my story was boring, and that nobody would find anything in it. Somehow, despite my nagging thoughts, I still found the gusto to write it. And I'm incredibly glad I did.

While looking back, I do think there were a few points I could have written better, I really, truly would never take back writing my first book. If anything, I hope that it makes people understand that they don't have to hold it in—that they can tell their stories, no matter how rough they are, and they can make something from them. Maybe even better than mine. However, truly, saying one story is better than the other is ridiculous—all stories are different and powerful, as long as it is an honest portrayal.

My favorite part of every signing is when people come up to me and share their stories. This exchange of stories—open and honest—is what makes every minute of this experience worth it. Often, simply because of the subject the book deals with, people who previously had no idea what the book was about will open up to me about their struggles, what they have encountered, and what they are doing to try to build from their own unique rubbles. This exchange helps me reevaluate how I'm coping with my own trauma, and I hope my story can do the same for others. I think it's the right time for this in our culture—like so many other things, we're realizing that sometimes it's better to talk about things rather than ignore the elephants in the room.

It also is telling that so many people *truly want* to talk about it, but feel they need to have that specific safe space to talk. And I get that, completely. That was the entire point of my first book—I never felt like I could talk about it because I feared that doing so would be a burden to those around me, and that they would get what I felt was "unnecessarily worried about me." Because I didn't give myself the time to find my own safe space, I harbored these thoughts within—I shouldered them on my own.

Obviously, as you could tell from my first book, I totally had it under control. Completely. 100% had it in the bag, you guys. Conquered that grief. Nobody had to worry for a minute about me.

(I hope you realize I'm joking. I realize I was a mess, and I'm fortunate that I found the strength to pull myself out, with the help of those I care about the most.)

Especially where I'm from—the Midwest, borderline rustbelt (Milwaukee)—being open and honest about how you're feeling is often seen as a weakness. While nobody would ever say that openly (we're *far* too repressed for that), it's telling that where I'm from, it's taboo to see a therapist. When you're seeing a therapist, the common response is, "Are you okay?" or simply "Why?" Where I'm from, the stoic repression of emotions is seen as a strength, not something that could actually hurt you in the long run. I don't think this is unique to Milwaukee, though it may manifest in different ways in different cities.

One thing I have struggled with whenever someone asks what my first book is about—I soften the actual premise. I usually say, "After my boyfriend passed, I went on a series of road trips following the last band we saw together." I feel, by saying that he simply passed, by keeping it vague, this shelters the person from an awkward or uncomfortable experience. But there's always the awkward and inevitable, "Oh, I'm so sorry. How did he pass?" where I then have to say it anyway. I still have to say, "Suicide." I usually try to soften the blow with saying, "He was always so self-sufficient," which I've learned is a very dark joke for someone who has just been surprised with that sort of information. This does not soften the blow, at all, ever, but for whatever reason, it always feels like the right thing to say there. It never is the right thing to say. Ever.

It wasn't until I was speaking with the head of NAMI Boston about my flyer for a signing in their city. Point blank, she asked, "If this is about suicide, why don't you say anything about it?" We had talked extensively over the phone and email about being honest about our stories, and by her calling me out on this, I immediately realized that *she was right*. While I had made it a point to be honest about everything else, I still felt the need to shelter others from the entire premise of my book. Obviously, they would find out eventually if they bought my book. Past that, in order to own my story, I had to actually *tell* it. *All* of it.

One of my favorite books is Elaine Scarry's *On Beauty and Being Just*, where she explains that true art comes from deep within the soul, authentic and pure. The more times it's copied and transposed on its surface, the more it loses its integrity. With each surface-level deviation I made on top of my life story, it lost its shine, which made me think I simply wasn't interesting when my false story didn't resonate. I didn't realize that it was worth telling simply because I transposed it and copied surface-level details—it wasn't interesting because I was too scared to show my soul, too scared to actually tell the truth.

One thing I've been working on this year is owning my own story—even its darkest recesses. This goes beyond the entire Jake story, to my deepest other stories, as everyone has. These stories that build our morals and shape the way we see the world—often times, they're learned the hard way, and sometimes opening up about them is a good way to process how you choose to react to these deeper, darker moments. Often times, people who have had similar stories react to them in different ways. And often times, you can learn from these reactions.

I would never go out of my way to tell people that my boyfriend committed suicide, unsolicited. If it is explicitly asked, I should own it as best I can. If anything, if they purchase the book, they're going to find out what happened anyway. It's not the most subtle about what happened—it's pretty to the point.

However, if you're shouting it to a room full of people who don't know you, unsolicited, you obviously haven't fully come to terms with it in your head. You need to open this topic internally and externally—you can't expect others to figure out your problems for you, especially if you sneak-attack them with problems at level 11. You have to accept it yourself before you can expect others to; any other way simply wouldn't be fair, especially because they will never fully know the story better than you.

Above all else, you should be open about your story. You should be true to yourself. However, you should also learn to process your story, both internally and externally. Simply telling your story—that's only half the battle. It's learning how to truly *own* your story before you expect others to own and accept it themselves.

Once I was able to begin to clear these blocks out of my head, I found that I actually enjoyed sharing my story—but even past that, I enjoyed leaving my apartment again. I enjoyed returning to the things in life that I previously enjoyed. I looked forward to going to a show, out to dinner, or for a walk with friends. I found that once I wasn't creating a performance every time I left my house, there was so much less stress. Once I began to be honest with myself, I could have fun again. I could really live again.

Building Beyond the Person You Lost (Without Blocking Them Out)

For so long, everything about moving on felt taboo. I mentioned this before, but want to touch on it again.

I felt that, to grieve properly, I needed to cling to him to retain his memory. As I mentioned in the first book, I thought this meant physically visiting his grave. This is something I'm still not able to do.

I thought this meant that, for the rest of my days, I wasn't allowed to date, because if I moved on, this meant (in my mind) that I was moving on from him, forgetting about him.

With time, I've learned this is not the case. To be a functioning human being, you cannot continue to cling to your past, no matter what your past is. You have to keep challenging yourself. You have to accept that desire to go out into the world and accept love again—for yourself and from others.

The thing was, at first, when I recognized I was feeling better again, I forced myself to feel worse—a never-ending, self-loathing cycle. As humans, we all experience light and darkness; even in our darkest moments, a good bowl of perfectly cinnamon-ed oatmeal can bring us joy, if only for a minute. For me, at a certain point in my grieving, I would mentally self-flagellate myself every time I felt any sort of happiness until I was back to my lowest point again. In my mind, if I were to feel happy at all, this meant that I wasn't sad enough, that I hadn't cared enough about him when I knew he felt nothing, when I knew that he had suffered. In effect, I was extending the last part of his legacy. It was extreme pain. I carried on this pain for him—though I know if he was here, this isn't what he'd want me to do.

I clung to the idea that I needed to make everything better—that I needed to right all wrongs—for too long. This held up my recovery process because I was so hyper-focused on making sure everyone else was okay without making sure *I* was okay. This manifested itself outside of those I encountered at home, my stable relationships, to those I met during my travels. If I sensed even the smallest amount of discomfort, I would go to great lengths to make sure that they felt okay even when I felt awful.

It always seems easier to care for others than to care for yourself because once people are out of sight, they have to deal with their problems on their own. But caring for yourself? You are with yourself all the time. If you hurt, you cannot walk away from that. The only way you can move forward is self-care; otherwise, you get stuck in that pain. Caring for others above yourself is pious, and what we are told is the true ideal of how to be a functioning member of society. And absolutely, you should help other people—I believe it is the most powerful form of therapy. But it must be balanced with taking care of yourself. You cannot reach out to someone from the bottom of the well, or if you're both there, a hug at the bottom of the well doesn't get you back to the top. The only way you can really help someone is if *you* are in a good place. You cannot give yourself wholly if you're not whole yourself.

It wasn't until I cut myself a break that I truly began to be a good person. In some ways, on the surface, the ways I did this made me look like a bad person. I stopped volunteering so much. I stopped going out as much. My social circle grew smaller. I spent more time on myself, time I used to spend on others.

With every night I spent with a cheap Egyptian clay face mask re-reading the same Guy Delisle graphic novel—the one on Jerusalem—my mind unwound from what I should be doing to what I am *currently* doing. By appreciating the present, I'm able to be more present than I was before. Because my brain was relaxed rather than wired on "I should be doing something," it worked better.

Before, I was hyper-focused on being a good person. I made sure that if someone needed help, I was the first line of defense. Even if I wasn't the right person for the job, I would force myself to be, even if I didn't have the time or the mentality necessary for it. One of many examples of this would be when I took a remote editing job for an online women's interest magazine—I was editing a slew of articles each week on topics I had no interest in, such as, "Which tampons are the best for those with wide cervixes?" and "What balayage hairstyle best fits your unique personality?" and "What to do if your man still hasn't popped the question?". I couldn't do a good job because, simply, I did not give a shit about what I was doing, but I convinced myself it's what I *should* be doing. (I ended up getting fired from this job, the first and only time I was ever fired, which was probably for the best, to be honest.)

I was wired to think that I should be doing something at all times, and this job was *something*, even though it wasn't necessarily enjoyable or the best use of my time. I wasn't comfortable when my plate wasn't full, mostly because then I had time to think about what I truly should be doing, instead of some other *something* to fill my time. The list could go on and on with examples of this, but this is the one that comes to mind first.

I would sacrifice my own personal life to ensure others could have theirs, because in my mind, they deserved it more than I did. In my mind, I could handle it; therefore, I should do it. When I heard others complain about how busy they were, I would focus on how to alleviate that stress rather than thinking about how stressed this would make me. I never stopped to think about when I would get a break—I was hyper-focused on making sure everyone else got theirs.

Granted, my break from this was forced. After Jake died, there was no way I could continue this work regimen because I wasn't able to do as much—at first, I was in inpatient, where I literally didn't have access to the outside world, and I was unable to work or to communicate with those outside of the hospital. Past that, depression kept me from leaving my apartment, or even my bed. I wasn't able to make the connections necessary to keep my plate full.

As I mentioned previously, I had an excellent therapist while in inpatient who taught me that many of my emotions are normal, and that I should analyze them as I feel them. For as long as I can remember, I've struggled with anxiety, which is a double-edged sword. This drove me to constantly be working on something—convincing myself that if I'm not doing something, I'm not doing anything, and that I'm worthless. I was used to working at 100% for so long because I was driven by my anxiety and that fear of being worthless, so I was used to the stress that accompanied this.

She explained to me that those suffering with anxiety disorders are used to operating at a "cup-near-overflowing" level—a level far past what a normal person would consider "overwhelming" simply because we're used to being overwhelmed by even the most minute aspects of life. This makes me sound superhuman, but also you have to consider that those who are not suffering from an anxiety disorder still have room left in their cup if they add any sort of stress in their lives. If you are only operating at 75%, you still have room in your cup if you realize you have to fill up your gas tank even if you have to be downtown in 15 minutes—meaning you will not have an anxiety attack at a seemingly small inconvenience. Because the average mind still allows itself room for more stresses, the anxious mind forces me to work at 100%, which does not allow for any unexpected deviations. Everything has to work exactly as I plan it to; otherwise, I melt down. My cup would immediately overflow, and I wouldn't be able to contain it with even the smallest deviation.

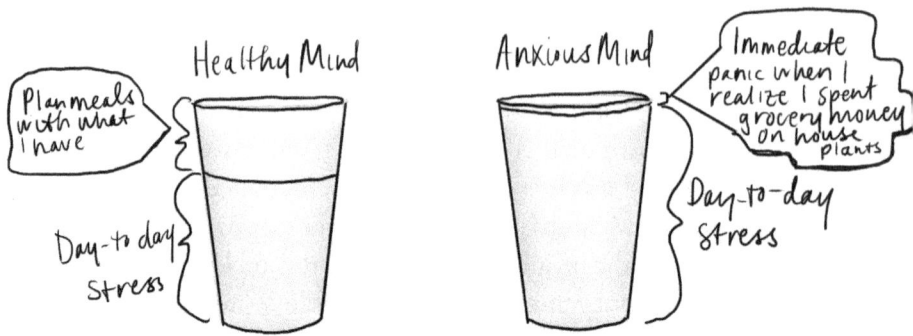

Because operating at 75% is not normal for me, I've had to force myself to relax once in a while. It's been difficult for me to realize that sometimes the best thing I can do for others is to care for myself. When operating at 100% all of the time, even self-care is enough to throw me into an anxiety attack (which, obviously, turned into more anxiety as things built up in my apartment, like laundry and dishes). I didn't give myself time to take care of the things I needed so I could care for myself, so because I was hyper-focused on helping everyone else, my ability to truly help people dwindled. If you're only half present, it's near impossible to truly help someone, as I wanted to do—or to help yourself, as I should have been doing, simply because your brain is not working at its full potential. You will never be your best version if you're constantly working at 100%, if you're moving from one anxiety attack to another. If you do not stop to care for yourself—if you do not spend a few days at a 50% anxiety level, serenading your cats with and dancing along to a Sonny Cleveland album in your living room (or whatever it is you do when you're trying to unwind)—you will ultimately suffer.

As I've mentioned in previous essays, I've forced myself to take a walk every day. This helps to unwind my mind—it's a set time where I don't have to do anything except move forward and meditate on what I will be doing that day. For me, this is a daily treat I give myself. It seems small, but in the past, I would have simply woken up and gone to work right away—immediately diving into the things I have to do for other people instead of doing something for myself. But because I start the day for me, this builds context onto the rest of my day. I'm mentally clearer because I took the time to care for myself first thing, rather than putting it off for later (then inevitably procrastinating on self-care).

And it's difficult—it's difficult to fully process that, to be a good person, you do need to spend time caring for yourself. For me, this didn't process until I started helping others with a well-rested brain, rather than one wracked with thinking "I should be doing all of these things because I should be doing things." Doing good comes more naturally when you *feel* good. Instead of simply being another task to accomplish, it's easier to help someone truly if your mind is in it. It can't truly be "in it" if you aren't fully focused, aren't fully there.

To me, it still feels odd to say, "The only way you can be a good person is if you first take care of yourself." I still suffer with the thoughts of "I should be doing something for others, because I'm strong and I can handle these stresses better." (And this may or may not be true—I can only speak from my own personal feelings; therefore, I have no idea how others process these stresses).

By admitting that, possibly, maybe, I can feel better if I choose to take care of myself while still caring for others, I've found I feel more rested on the same amount of sleep. By caring for myself, I'm learning to love myself as much as I love and respect those around me, those I want to help. And I realized that I, too, was worthy of being helped, and that what I was doing was also great (at least, if I spent the time necessary to cultivate my own projects, rather than wondering how I could help others with theirs.) I've learned how to respect myself while still respecting those around me—a balance I have to work on, but with each day, it seems to come more naturally. I'm able to be influenced by others simply because I'm working on myself and with others—and this encourages me, and help keeps me grounded.

CHAPTER TEN
THE FIGHT

The moment I decided to write this second book, I debated whether I would include this. It's an incredibly sensitive discussion that really lays myself bare in front of people who, I feel, ultimately would not understand it and would immediately vilify me once they read it.

But the point of this book is to move forward, and to do that, I have to accept the entire story and lay it bare in front of all of you as readers, no matter how you may interpret it. I cannot hide it from you anymore if I want to healthfully move forward.

I cheated on him.

I'm not proud of it, and if I had been in the same situation again, in my current mind, of course it wouldn't have happened.

But it did.

For so long, I hid from this, but it would inevitably come out as my conscience lured it out—even if it was only myself, wracked by guilt, with harsh light casting down on my sleep-deprived face in my bathroom mirror at 2:00 am. My body was exhausted, but my mind would re-live the decisions leading up to this. I never thought that I would ever forgive myself for these weak moments leading up to these decisions. But I have. Slowly, but surely, I have.

I do not condone my actions. I admit they were the actions of a weak character. I am fortunate that I have grown past this weak character. However, I do feel since you have been with me for this long, I owe you at least this much to tell you this very intimate detail. And I feel the only way to continue to build away from this is to admit what I did wrong, to acknowledge it as openly as I can, and learn to move forward from there in a more positive direction.

But let me explain how I got to this point.

We were not perfect. Neither of us. It's often said that broken people will find each other, but when we found each other, we were not broken. We were too young to be fully broken—at 17, you own the world, even if the world isn't going exactly the way you want it to. In these first few years, we shared everything—jokes, dreams, and lots and lots of coffee and breakfast sandwiches.

But as we got older, we did not adjust our relationship to fit our newfound worldviews. Separately, we became broken. We tried to hide this from each other. He—he was dealing with he early stages of bipolar. Me—I was dealing with poor self-esteem issues that I've harbored since a child, and the need to make everyone around me happy before myself.

It's difficult to be in a relationship with someone who is slowly losing his mind, but equally difficult to be with someone who is constantly battling self-esteem issues. And my issues were much more deep seeded—they weren't the external "I feel fat today," at all. They were of my self-worth, feeling worthless, feeling useless. As soon as you feel those things, you do not seek out healthy relationships. You seek out temporary relationships because ultimately, you do not see yourself worthy of love. You break it off before you have to deal with anything— that is at least how I manufactured it in my mind, even if I didn't realize this at the time.

But with Jake, above everything else, he was my best friend. My confidant. And even though he was my confidant, I hid this from him. I respected him so much that I did not want any chance of losing him, so I pretended everything was going great while harboring a separate life to keep myself going, to try to build a solid base out of eggshells. And I admit it seems strange to say "I respected him" while also going behind his back, but when the mind is frantic, these now-obvious connections didn't seem obvious at the time. My mind was on self-preservation—it was finding any sort of stability in an otherwise unstable condition.

When I realized I couldn't make him happy, instead of sitting down and having the very necessary discussion I should have had, I fled and sought shelter with someone else. I felt guilty asking him to do this for me because in my eyes, I was not worthy of this from him.

I held him on a pedestal for so long, and I think at least for the beginning of our relationship, he deserved it. He was an incredibly strong person, with quick wit and a kind heart. Again, I don't want to speak for him, but I believe he did the same for me. We adored each other, and in those first few years, we knew each other more intimately than I've known anyone. When I realized that this pedestal was flawed, that I had crafted him into some godly figure instead of the very human figure that he was, I was scared. I blamed myself. Instead of retreating, he lashed out because he saw I wasn't living up to the potential he saw for me in his mind. (At least, that's how I interpret it, now. Again, I can't speak for him.)

I flaked, to put it lightly and bluntly.

The worst part is that he found out not from me, but from reading my diary.

This part—this is something I will never forgive myself for, and I actually think that's a good thing because hopefully, that will ensure that I am never in this situation again. I think this was, again, the actions of a weak character, but also actions that cannot be condoned. Even after it happened, I realized I couldn't keep it from him forever. But time seems to go on for an eternity until it doesn't. Time is finite. I waited for the right time to tell him, but obviously, with this kind of thing, there is no "right time."

There is never a right time for tough conversations, which I think is what makes them the most difficult to have. What is most difficult to realize when you're trying to find the perfect time to tell something to anyone is you don't have time—the longer you wait, the longer it festers in your mind. And the more secrets you keep to cover up this initial lie.

But I hope by admitting it, I can give a very human face to a very humanly weak decision. I hope that you can learn from what I did and apply it to your own relationships. Even if it's spilling wine on your brand-new white carpet—your partner is going to find out eventually. Even if it's feeding the wrong food to your best friend's dog while she is on vacation—it'll come up eventually if that dog is truly as sensitive as she says it is. The strongest thing you can do is to take a deep breath and admit what you did wrong—to confess without defenses up, to be vulnerable in front of your partner or whoever it is you wronged. It's terrifying, and many times, the actions leading to this are incredibly flawed, but these flaws are human and cannot be avoided. They only fester more the longer they are pushed to the side. And it's possible they may reject you, and this is terrifying, too—I know firsthand because it was this very fear of rejection that kept me from admitting my wrongs to Jake.

But at least you have the peace of mind that you were honest and sincere leading up to it. Life is vulnerable, visceral, and entirely too short to spend it hiding secrets from those you care about—even if your secrets contain your flaws. Those who love you love you fully, but they can only love you fully if you *give* yourself fully, honestly, truly. You owe this to them.

While I have forgiven myself for this, it does not mean I do not still regret this. I do—wholly. I regret that I involved people who should not have been involved in the first place. I regret what I did to him. But I cannot continue to self-flagellate with self-deprecating thoughts. I cannot continue to live in the past and to continue to hate myself for these actions.

I have to move forward from this simply by learning, and by promising myself to do better going forward. The person I know I can and should be. The person I have become.

CHAPTER ELEVEN
HEALING THE STIGMA

Let me get one thing as honest and as clear as possible—after I've opened up about what has happened to me, I am not allowed to have a sad day, ever, without a few people growing concerned that I'm regressing. I'm not allowed to have a bad day, a sad day, or even a mediocre day. Even though I went into this with minor, manageable depression, that has been wiped clean from everyone's memory after 2016. Every sad day is connected to Jake now, though many times it has nothing to do with him. Even if it's just "I'm sad because I didn't get enough sleep last night and I'm also sad that there are no peanut butter cups in my house," it's difficult to convince people that you're okay unless you're happy 100% all of the time. You are now on a *sadness pedestal* that some people are now convinced they cannot reach, and can never understand. Because I faced an admittedly horrific tragedy, this tends to alienate some people who I once held close.

That's okay, and I've grown to accept that and move forward.

Though I've moved past it, I also want to say that for the average person, nobody is happy 100% of the time. Most of the time, we're decent, which there's nothing wrong with. In fact, right now, I'm going on a crusade to rebrand *decent* as a perfectly acceptable mood to be in because it's honest and it's homeostasis and it's humble. But for some people, they want you to be *better* than good. They want you to be *great*. And while their heart is in the right place, this just sometimes isn't completely possible. And to be honest, it's not something I would want for myself. To be perfectly honest with you, being great 100% of the time sounds exhausting.

This can be frustrating, especially as someone who is often told to "smile more." And this was even before 2016—when I was in Germany in 2011 visiting Jake, who was studying in Frankfurt for a year, I had an old man yell at me in German for not smiling on Christmas, probably something akin to *Lachle mehr!*, which is the last thing I want to hear in any context, even if it has to be translated to me. I was actually in a great mood at the time. I was over the moon about seeing the love of my life after a six-month break in a new country, excited to see his new world, excited to experience it with him for a month. That didn't matter. (I guess my face tends to scream *not happy*, no matter what my mood is.)

This has caused me to lie about how I'm feeling—to instead say, "I'm great!" even if I felt like a sack of shit that fell out of the back of a Toyota Yaris that was then was run over by a semi-truck, and that then hit the cement divider on the highway in one dramatic, defeated splat. Even *then*, I would fake a smile and pretend like everything was great. This is exactly what I'm trying to avoid doing now, as this mood repression is what fueled my manic quest for reason in 2017.

For me, blunt honesty is what I need, but this is not the way to approach everyone. This is not the way to tell everyone how you feel, which sucks, but it's honest. There is a way to be honest with those who may treat you differently, though, much like my rebranding of *decent*—it's to put it in a different light.

You cannot expect someone to understand your hurt if you do not give the entire picture, and if you attack that person with your pain. Like I mentioned before, by honestly sharing and letting your vulnerabilities show, and by being open to suggestions and discussion, this tends to help me explain how I am feeling to people without that wall of tragedy covering my words. Sometimes, this internal rebranding as I'm talking with others helps me process it in my own mind. If I cast it in a new light instead of exposing it in its raw, gritty, unprocessed form—if I process my thoughts internally before I let them out externally—I've found I'm able to connect with people much better, despite that wall.

Of course, nobody can fully understand your pain because they are not living in your brain—they can never know the nuances as well as you do unless you lay them out.

This obviously does not work for everyone—not everyone will understand your hardships, especially if you haven't completely processed them in your brain yourself. That's okay. It's difficult—I'm not saying it's not. And, again, I feel like I sound like a broken record when I say, "It's okay," but I mean it. *It's okay*. It's better than pretending to be okay and shouldering this burden yourself.

With that stigma that surrounds those who have openly struggled, or those who have experienced tragedy—at times, I've kept what has happened to me, for fear of how others will react. For me, especially because I am trying to rebuild my world outside of my struggle and my book, it's difficult when someone finds out what I'm doing through word of mouth or through a flyer—suddenly, that dynamic changes.

Those who have suffered have time to process those struggles in their minds. Those who have not experienced those struggles have not had time to process—so it makes sense for them to suddenly feel nervous or confused.

That dynamic always changes once someone figures out what happened, which is natural, because all of us put ourselves in someone else's shoes when we hear about their struggles. And foreign struggles always seem worse when happening to someone else—when you're not the one suffering from them, when you're not the one who has experienced them firsthand.

This dynamic shift is human. Those around you—there's no way they can understand your pain or how you deal with that. If they are trying to make you feel better, even if it doesn't work, you should acknowledge that their heart is in the right place and try to better explain what works for you in the future, instead of cutting them out completely, as I did to some of those in my life. This is something I will probably never forgive myself for, in my weakest days, but I have moved past it and I have learned from it—some of these relationships I can't rebuild, but I've luckily been able to learn from that. Fortunately, not everyone has been through the same things I have been through, so I've had a lot of these encounters.

This is what makes us human—our need to connect and to help those around us, to build our relationships around us. Instead of seeing someone as ignorant, see it as vulnerable and human, while still exposing them to how you feel respectfully. Remember that by reaching out to you, they are putting themselves in a vulnerable position as well.

I completely get it—this is something I used to do. I used to be the person to ask, "But are you okay, *really?*" To be clear, I do not hate the people who do this, but at the same time, it does make me feel uncomfortable. However, it has to be addressed that those who are reaching out to you feel equally uncomfortable. Much like they can't read your mind, you also cannot read theirs.

You are not your past. You are who you are, present. Unless you cling to your past, you are your present self, and only you can define yourself. But you cannot expect those around you to understand this immediately—this is something you have to explain to them.

Don't shut them out—guide them on how they can help. Remove that stigma by actively showing others how to.

Chapter Twelve

"What Should I Say to Someone Who Has Lost Someone to Suicide?"

This is the most common question I've been asked after writing my first book—and the one I feel is the most difficult to answer. I want to reiterate that everyone is different, that everyone processes everything differently, and that what worked for me may not work for your niece, your best friend, or whoever else you're wondering on how to approach.

In my opinion, the emphasis shouldn't be on what you say to them. You should only say something if they bring it up to you, and to simply be a vessel for listening, rather than trying to offer advice. At least for me, when I was in the peak of processing, the last thing I wanted to do was to re-live the trauma while in public. If I finally pulled myself out of my apartment, that meant I was looking for an escape. I didn't want to rehash my traumas; the few times I did, I would bring it up first (even when I didn't know how to, or even when it was awkward). When I did want to talk about it, I would.

The emphasis shouldn't be on getting them to talk about it—it should be about knowing that if they want to talk about it, you're there for them, wholly. Support is the most important thing during these times, as well as reminding those who are suffering that there is a world outside of their trauma. Be kind to them—include them in plans, knowing fully that they may cancel last-minute if they're having a rough day. Don't hate them for it if they do, or if they do ghost, the emphasis should be on letting them know they aren't abandoned.

After Jake passed the way he did, I feared that if he could leave that suddenly, my other relationships would, too. I started to process my relationships differently, assuming that everyone would leave eventually. My closest friends now are not the ones who asked me how I was doing on a daily basis. My closest friends were the ones who would send me stupid cat memes, who would rehash embarrassing memories we've shared together, or would talk with me about their crushes, just as they had before. Those people didn't change—they were reminders that I still had solid, unwavering relationships out there, rather than a dynamic shift.

It's difficult—I get it. In these situations, I tend to mother-hen, to smother, to try to fix all of the problems for this person. There is no simple fix to an incredibly complex situation like this—there are so many different aspects associated with it, which makes it difficult to truly understand the situation. You can't give answers without knowing the situation fully, and there's no way you can ever know the situation as completely as the person who is suffering. For me, it was this trauma, and I was also dealing with the aftermath of what was, on both sides, a very unhealthy relationship. There is no way anyone could have known about this simply because I hadn't told anyone, so any advice people would give to me unsolicited always seemed forced because it wasn't fully grasping the entire situation. It didn't seem applicable because I didn't feel comfortable giving them all of the information, at least not at that time.

There were often times I felt pressured to talk with people about it, simply because they asked about it and I could tell they wanted me to talk about it. I found myself faking emotions I knew they felt I should process at that time, based off of what I knew they expected me to feel. But much like any instance in life, when you're actually going through something, often times the processing stage is much different than you could have ever anticipated. And the only way to process it is simply by going through it. I never hated anyone for trying to anticipate how I was processing this incredibly traumatic situation, but it did make me feel alienated when I felt others were putting me on a trauma pedestal. It was hard—the only thing I truly needed at that time was to be included, to be accepted, to be told, "That sucks, but the rest of your world is still there, and that's not changing anytime soon."

Again, I understand this question, and I understand this question comes from a good place. The one thing I want to emphasize is that neither of us know what to do. There is no answer on how to feel better because there *is* no way to feel better in this incredibly traumatic situation. The best thing you can say? "That sucks," followed by consistently supporting them as you had before. An unchanging approach to the relationship is far more impactful than any words could say. The world of this person has just been rocked in a way that is difficult to comprehend, meaning any sort of personal familiarities will help this person realize that there is a world outside of trauma. Even if it's taking that person to her favorite restaurant for free chips and salsa—often times, any sort of reminder that there is a world outside of trauma is the best thing you can do for someone who has been through something similar.

I'm speaking for what was best for me. Again, this could be different for your niece, your sister-in-law, your friend. But for me, any sort of reminder of the world outside of myself was what I needed. When others hyper-focused on that trauma, that was when I felt trapped, when I felt the need to retreat. But it was when others took me for walks in parks I've been talking about visiting but never have, or sent me stupid articles from *The Onion*, or invited me to comedy shows, all while being patient if I was having a difficult day and canceled—this unchanging support was much more powerful than anything anyone could have ever said to me.

Epilogue

Here, now. March 24, 2019. In three weeks, I will be completely done with my tour with book one, and I'm finally starting to understand how to organize a tour on my own. I'm finally starting to fully learn how to own my story authentically, rather than as a set story I wrote in 2018, rather than distancing it as something that had happened in my past. I'm finally starting to understand that the story I wrote last year is dynamic, ever-changing, and that it will continue to build as I continue to process. I've learned how to share this with others—with those I cherish the most, and with those I've just met.

I had hoped that once the tour ended, I would be able to distance myself from it, that I would move on from it fully—but as I'm learning in these last few stops, that's never going to be the case. It will *always* be a part of me. It will continue to be a part of both my private and public life, and I'm learning how to mesh that into my life moving ahead, sustainably and productively. The purpose of this book is to describe how I'm moving forward—and much like my first book, this one will also continue to grow, far beyond these final pages.

In my last book, I told you about the cut and burn I got on my arm—a scar of Rush's *Snakes and Arrows* tour symbol. While my scar artist has assured me it is still healing healthfully, the process has been delayed by hypertrophic scarring (if you Google it, the images look far worse than mine do, but it's still not exactly friendly for short sleeves). It's funny—my mom had a scar on her leg that started to hypertrophic scar. Apparently, it's something that runs in our family (excess collagen buildup with particularly traumatic injuries, whether they're self-induced or by some camping accident, like with my mom's). And from what I've seen, this doesn't happen often. I'm part of a small percentage of potential side effects.

Much in my last book, I'll overanalyze this attribute of mine. I had said my scar would heal within the year, but unexpectedly, it grew and morphed into something else. My scar artist and an ER doctor I saw in a panic both assure me that, by applying silicone scar sheets to it, the swelling should reduce, and it should look normal within a few months (and it seems to be working, as it looks much better after just a month), but much like I describe in this book, no healing process is normal. There will always be hiccups, but it's about owning these, addressing these, and dealing with these hiccups properly, instead of hiding them underneath long sleeves or masks.

I hope to continue to heal, both mentally and physically. I hope that this journey continues to be as fruitful and as fulfilling as it has been in the past year. I hope my story helps you, and I hope that someday, you can tell me your story, so I can grow from that, too.

Moving forward? I will continue to work on owning my story, wholly. When someone asks me what happened, I will work on sharing the situation without lying. I hope to continue to be honest about who I am and where I came from and where I'm going. And I hope to continue to choose to become the person I know I can grow into. Who I know I can be.

That said, while it's been fun to share my story with you—and I hope you were able to get something from it—I think I'm going to go back to writing fiction, now.

There's an idea I've been meaning to flesh out since before any of this happened—an idea scrawled onto notebook paper in 2013. It was set aside when I broke my foot while working on a production floor in 2013. It was set aside again when I got a new job, and my job got too intense from 2014–2015. And it was set aside again when my car was stolen (my notebooks and flash drives with all of my work were, conveniently, stored in my back seat) in 2016. Then of course, after Jake passed, I needed to repair myself. And so it was set aside again. While I am not writing this next idea for him, it has been in the back of my mind all this time, and this was the first idea that he said, "Yeah, I think you could probably go somewhere with that." (He was my toughest critic, but again, I appreciate him for that.)

Now that I think I'm in a good spot again (knock on wood), I think it's finally time to return to that idea—*Death's Intern Derrick*.

www.ingramcontent.com/pod-product-compliance
Lightning Source LLC
Chambersburg PA
CBHW031630040426

42452CB00007B/762